THE SLEEP

THE SLEEPING PRINCE

An Occasional Fairy Tale

by
TERENCE RATTIGAN

SAMUEL  FRENCH

LONDON
NEW YORK TORONTO SYDNEY HOLLYWOOD

Copyright 1954 by Terence Rattigan
© Acting Edition 1956 by Terence Rattigan

This play is fully protected under the copyright laws of the British Commonwealth of Nations, the United States of America, and all countries of the Berne and Universal Copyright Conventions.

All rights are strictly reserved.

It is an infringement of the copyright to give any public performance or reading of this play either in its entirety or in the form of excerpts without the prior consent of the copyright owners. No part of this publication may be transmitted, stored in a retrieval system, or reproduced in any form or by any means, electronic, mechanical, photocopying, manuscript, typescript, recording, or otherwise, without the prior permission of the Copyright owners.

SAMUEL FRENCH LTD, 26 SOUTHAMPTON STREET, STRAND, LONDON, WC2, or their authorized agents, issue licences to amateurs to give performances of this play on payment of a fee. **The fee must be paid, and the licence obtained, before a performance is given.**

Licences are issued subject to the understanding that it shall be made clear in all advertising matter that the audience will witness an amateur performance; and that the names of the authors of plays shall be included in all announcements and on all programmes.

The royalty fee indicated below is subject to contract and subject to variation at the sole discretion of Samuel French Ltd.

> Fee for each and every
> performance by amateurs   **Code H**
> in the British Isles

In territories overseas the fee quoted above may not apply. A quotation will be given upon application to the authorized agents, or direct to Samuel French Ltd.

ISBN 0 573 01421 3

Please note our NEW ADDRESS:

Samuel French Ltd
52 Fitzroy Street London W1P 6JR
Tel: 01 - 387 9373

THE SLEEPING PRINCE

Concerning (in strict order of precedence) the following personages:

HIS MAJESTY KING NICOLAS VIII OF CARPATHIA

HIS ROYAL HIGHNESS, THE GRAND DUKE CHARLES, PRINCE REGENT OF CARPATHIA

HER IMPERIAL AND ROYAL HIGHNESS, THE GRAND DUCHESS CHARLES

HER ROYAL HIGHNESS, THE ARCHDUCHESS FERDINAND OF STYRIA

HER ROYAL HIGHNESS, THE PRINCESS LOUISA OF STYRIA

COUNT TRIGORINSKY, major-domo to the Grand Duke

THE COUNTESS VON UND ZU MEISSENBRONN, lady-in-waiting to the Grand Duchess

THE HONOURABLE PETER NORTHBROOK, attached to the Grand Duke's suite

THE BARONESS BRUNHEIM, lady-in-waiting to the Grand Duchess

BARON SCHWARTZ, butler to the Grand Duke

FREIHERR VON BRAUN, personal footman to the Grand Duke

UR DE GRUNE, personal footman to the Grand Duke

MISS MARY MORGAN, whose stage name (to avoid confusion) is ELAINE DAGENHAM

THE SLEEPING PRINCE

Presented by H. M. Tennent Ltd at The Phoenix Theatre, London, on the 5th November 1953, with the following cast of characters:

(in the order of their appearance)

1st Footman	*Angus Mackay*
2nd Footman	*Terence Owen*
Peter	*Richard Wattis*
Mary	*Vivien Leigh*
The Major-Domo	*Paul Hardwick*
The Butler	*Peter Barkworth*
The Regent	*Laurence Olivier*
Nicolas	*Jeremy Spenser*
The Grand Duchess	*Martita Hunt*
The Countess	*Rosamund Greenwood*
The Baroness	*Daphne Newton*
The Archduchess	*Elaine Inescort*
Louisa	*Nicola Delman*

The play directed by Laurence Olivier

Setting designed by Roger Furse

SYNOPSIS OF SCENES

The action of the play passes in the Royal Suite of the Carpathian Legation in Belgrave Square, London

ACT I

Scene 1 Wednesday, 21st June 1911, about 11.30 p.m.
Scene 2 8.30 the following morning

ACT II

Scene 1 About 7 p.m. of the same day
Scene 2 About 12.30 the same night
Scene 3 10 a.m. the following morning

MUSIC

The barrel-organ music by Vivian Ellis from *The Cocoanut Girl* is published as a piano arrangement by Chappell & Co Ltd, 50, New Bond Street, London, W1 and is available from Samuel French.

Permission to perform the play does not include permission to use the words and music from *The Cocoanut Girl*.

Where the theatre or hall in which the play is being performed is licenced by the Performing Right Society a return must be made in the usual way; but where the theatre or hall is not so licenced permission must be sought from Messrs Chappell & Co Ltd.

THE SLEEPING PRINCE

ACT I

Scene 1

Scene—*The Royal Suite of the Carpathian Legation in Belgrave Square, London. Wednesday, 21st June 1911, about 11.30 p.m.*

We are looking at a very elegantly furnished octagonal room of which five walls are visible, the "fourth" wall in this case being, in fact, the sixth, seventh and eighth. Taking up the entire wall up L, *is a pair of massive double doors, leading to a corridor and thence to the main entrance and other parts of the building. There is a large window filling the wall up* R. *There are doors down* R *and* L *leading to bedrooms. Back* C *is an arched alcove. There are armchairs with footstools down* R *and* L *and a somewhat larger armchair stands* LC. *There is a sofa at a slight angle* RC *and a small circular table* C. *A desk and chair stand by the window and there are small tables* R *and* L. *The alcove is furnished with a large jardinière filled with mixed hydrangeas with a potted palm on a table behind it. At night the room is lit by wall-brackets, a chandelier and four table-lamps. On the table* C *there is a bell-push with a concealed cable, communicating with a bell in the corridor* L.

(*See the Ground Plan*)

When the Curtain *rises, the stage is empty, the window curtains are closed and all the lights are on. After a moment, the double doors are thrown open by the* 1st *and* 2nd Footmen, *who enter and stand on either side of the battants. They wear a distinctive livery.* The Honourable Peter Northbrook *follows the footmen on. He is aged about forty, is something in the Foreign Office and is, at the moment, attached to the Regent's suite. He is wearing tails.* Miss Mary Morgan, *whose stage name, to avoid confusion, is* Elaine Dagenham, *is seen to walk past the double doors and along the corridor. She is dressed in a very simple white evening dress, is young and considered very alluring. When she speaks it is with a fairly pronounced American accent.*

Peter (*as he enters*) Miss Dagenham, as I was saying . . . (*He realizes* Mary *is not there, breaks off, goes to the double doors, looks off and calls*) Miss Dagenham, this way, please. (*He stands above the doors*)

(Mary *enters by the double doors, crosses to* C *and then stands stockstill, looking about her in wonder*)

Mary (*looking around in awe*) Gosh!

(*The two* FOOTMEN *exit by the double doors*)

This is the first time I've ever seen the inside of an embassy.
PETER (*moving up* LC) Legation.

(*The two* FOOTMEN *close the double doors*)

MARY. Same thing, isn't it?
PETER (*moving behind the chair* LC) Not quite. There are only nine embassies in London at the present time.
MARY (*crossing to the chair down* R; *slightly disappointed*) Oh, you mean they don't rate Carpathia as all that important? (*She puts her wrap on the chair, then moves below the sofa*)
PETER. Not yet.
MARY. It looks enormous on the map.
PETER (*moving above the table* C *to* R *of the sofa*) Maps can be misleading.

(MARY *turns to watch Peter*)

Don't misunderstand me, Miss—er—Dagenham. I'm not, in any way, trying to belittle Carpathia. I've never been there, but I gather there is quite a lot to be said for the country. Its trains run on time—and its army, after France, Russia and Germany, is the best in Europe. What is more . . .
MARY. Pardon me. May I sit down?
PETER. Of course.

(MARY *gingerly settles herself on the sofa, at the right end, with evident pleasure*)

MARY. This is really something, isn't it?
PETER. Something?
MARY. This room and everything.
PETER (*looking around*) Yes. Personally I find the decorations a little vulgar.
MARY. Then give me vulgarity. Do you live here?
PETER. No. I am merely attached temporarily to the Grand Duke's suite. (*He crosses below the sofa to* R *of the chair* LC) There are, of course, similar appointments made for all the royal visitors to the Coronation, but in view of the recent adherence of Carpathia to the Entente Cordiale and the great importance attached by the Foreign Secretary to that adherence, a rather special appointment has been made in the case of the Grand Duke. (*He moves up* L) You see, I am actually the head of the Balkan Department at the Foreign Office.
MARY (*uninterested*) You don't say!

(PETER *crosses to* L)

Who's coming to this supper—apart from His Majesty, I mean?

PETER (*turning; startled*) His Majesty?
MARY. The Grand Duke.
PETER (*crossing to* L *of the sofa*) Oh. My dear, you quite startled me. Look, Miss Dagenham, as I gather you're a citizen of the United States, I think perhaps before the Grand Duke arrives— you should learn the correct form of address. Otherwise, who knows, there may be a few *petits moments d'embarras*.
MARY (*murmuring*) Now, I should just hate that.
PETER. The Grand Duke is not King of Carpathia, but Regent.
MARY. Same . . .
PETER (*interrupting*) No, it is *not* the same thing. (*He moves up* L *of the sofa*) The Grand Duke, who was a Prince of Hungary, married the late Queen of Carpathia and while she was alive had the title and form of Prince Consort. On her death their son, Nicolas—a minor—became King, and the Grand Duke was appointed Prince Regent. The correct form is therefore "Your Royal Highness".
MARY. I thought his wife was alive.
PETER. She is. (*He moves above the table* C) But it's his wife—*en secondes noces*.
MARY. What's that mean?
PETER (*after due thought*) His second wife.
MARY. Why isn't she Queen?
PETER (*moving down* L *of Mary*) Oh, for heaven's sake. It's perfectly simple . . .
MARY. Not to me.
PETER. Look, Miss Dagenham, I really don't think you need bother your very pretty little head——
MARY. Thank you.
PETER. —with abstruse questions of primogeniture and Salic Laws and things. Just remember that your host tonight—The Grand Duke Charles—is addressed as Your Royal Highness, or sir, that his wife, the Grand Duchess Charles, is addressed as Your Imperial and Royal Highness, or ma'am . . .
MARY (*rising*) Hi, wait a moment. That's a lot to remember. Imperial *and* Royal? Why all that?
PETER. That is far too complicated to explain. It all goes back to the Holy Roman Empire. She is a niece of the Emperor Franz Joseph.
MARY. No wisecracks about Austria, then?
PETER. I sincerely trust no wisecracks about anything, Miss Dagenham—of diplomatic moment, that is. In these troubled times the lightest remark can have terrible repercussions.
MARY. Gee! I can see the history books now. The war of Dagenham's Remark. (*She moves to* R *of the sofa and turns*)
PETER (*moving to* L *of the table* C) If you *should* meet the young King . . .
MARY. Oh, gosh! *Another* one?

PETER. He is addressed as Your Majesty, sire, or sir. Now have you got all that straight?

MARY (*moving up* R *of the sofa*) Gee. I don't think so. Altogether far too much plot in far too little time.

PETER (*puzzled*) Plot? (*He smiles politely*) Oh, yes, of course. A stage term. (*He moves to* L *of Mary*) Oh, and one other point. In conversation with royalty only speak when you are directly addressed.

MARY. You mean wait for the cue before speaking the line?

PETER (*moving behind the desk*) I suppose you could put it like that. (*He looks through the window curtains*)

MARY (*moving up* LC) Oh, God, I'm shaking. It's worse than a first night. (*She turns to him*) Do you think we've come to the right place? (*She moves up* L *and turns*) Where are the other guests?

PETER (*moving below the desk*) I don't know. I was told eleven-thirty. It's after that now.

MARY (*moving to* L *of the sofa*) But why am *I* asked anyway—do you know?

PETER. Well, after all you met him the other night, didn't you, when he came to your show?

MARY. Sure, but so did the ten other principals, and I was right at the end of the line.

PETER. It seemed to me that he paid you rather particular attention that night.

MARY. Well, now you mention it, it did strike me, I admit, that I was a couple of yesses and a no up on Laura Cardus, who was standing next to me. (*She moves below the chair* LC *and keeping an arm on it, circles it and stands above it*) But I can assure you our dialogue wasn't so brilliant that he must have felt he simply had to have that female Oscar Wilde to set his supper table in a roar tonight. (*She moves below the sofa*) Are you sure he hasn't mixed me up with Maisie?

PETER (*moving to* R *of the sofa*) Maisie?

MARY. Maisie Springfield, the leading lady. She's met him before, in Paris. She's always telling us.

PETER. No. I'm quite sure he means you.

MARY. But why—when I've only got that little bit in the second act?

PETER. Well—perhaps that was just the little bit he liked.

(*There is a pause.* MARY *paces down* L *of the chair* LC)

MARY. You know, this silence is getting me down. Apart from the other guests, where the heck is my host?

PETER. I don't know. Earlier he was due to have dinner with the Foreign Secretary.

MARY. What does he want supper for then?

PETER. The appetite of these Balkan royalties is often quite prodigious.

(*A sound is heard at the double doors*)

MARY (*in a frantic whisper*) Oh God! (*She crosses down* R) Here they come.

(PETER *moves up* L *of the desk*)

I only hope to heaven I know some of them. I hope there are about a hundred guests, then I can get lost.

(COUNT TRIGORINSKY, *major-domo to the Regent, enters by the double doors. He bows to Mary, imperiously signals to the* FOOTMEN, *then crosses and stands down* C. *The two* FOOTMEN *enter, carrying a small table which they place* C *of the sofa. The* 1ST FOOTMAN *is at the left end of the table, and the* 2ND FOOTMAN *is at the right end of it. They spread the cloth and set out the cutlery, under the supervision of the* MAJOR-DOMO. *The* BUTLER *enters by the double doors. He carries a tray with a silver cruet, two small bowls of roses and two napkins. He hands the tray to the* 1ST FOOTMAN. *The* MAJOR-DOMO *moves behind the Butler to up* C, *followed by the* 2ND FOOTMAN *who exits by the double doors. The* BUTLER *crosses below the table and stands behind it, bowing to Mary on the way. The* 1ST FOOTMAN *stands with the tray* L *of the Butler.* MARY *has her eyes riveted to the proceedings.* PETER *crosses to* L. *The* BUTLER *first takes the bowls of roses from the tray and places one in front of each place, then puts out the table napkins and finally, places the cruet* C *of the table. As soon as it becomes apparent that only two places are being laid,* MARY *tries to catch the attention of* PETER, *who is, rather studiedly, staring at a picture.* MARY *crosses below the table to* LC. PETER *crosses up* R *and moves to the desk.* MARY *crosses below the table towards Peter, but is stopped by the* MAJOR-DOMO *who is crossing down* R)

Hey! (*She darts behind the desk after Peter*)

(*The* MAJOR-DOMO *stands down* RC. *The* 1ST FOOTMAN *crosses to the double doors and exits with the tray. The* BUTLER *moves and stands above the table* C. *The* MAJOR-DOMO *crosses towards the double doors.* PETER *crosses down* L *with* MARY *in pursuit*)

Hey! (*She is again impeded by the Major-Domo and dodges round him*)

(*The* 2ND FOOTMAN *enters by the double doors. He carries a large silver salver with an ice-bucket containing a bottle of champagne and a smaller ice-bucket containing a bottle of vodka. The* 1ST FOOTMAN *enters by the double doors. He carries a silver salver with two champagne glasses and two vodka glasses. The* 2ND FOOTMAN *hands his tray to the* BUTLER, *who places it on the table* C. *The* 1ST FOOTMAN *holds out his tray to the* BUTLER *who takes the glasses and sets them on the supper table. The* 2ND FOOTMAN *moves and stands upstage of the double doors, and the* 1ST FOOTMAN *downstage of them*)

(*To Peter. Under her breath*) Hey!

(PETER *takes no notice. The* BUTLER *bows to the* MAJOR-DOMO, *then moves to the double doors*)

(*Louder*) Hey!

(PETER *turns to Mary*)

(*She moves to* R *of Peter and points frantically to the supper table*) Two places . . .
 PETER (*moving up* R; *out of the corner of his mouth*) Pas devant . . .
 MARY (*following Peter*) What?
 PETER (*out of the corner of his mouth*) Not in front of . . . (*He indicates the servants*)
 MARY (*frantically*) Yes—but *two* places.
 PETER (*crossing round the sofa and standing above the table* C; *peremptorily*) Sh!

(*The* BUTLER *turns and exits by the double doors. The two* FOOTMEN *follow him off. The* MAJOR-DOMO *crosses to the double doors, turns, bows, then turns and exits, closing the doors.* MARY *watches them off, then hurriedly collects her wrap and darts above the sofa towards the double doors*)

(*He intercepts Mary above the sofa and bars her way*) Please. I beg you, Miss Dagenham, control yourself. There's no need for panic.
 MARY. Isn't there just? This is a plot, isn't it—supper for two? You knew all about it.
 PETER. Well, I suppose I have to confess that I did have an idea—when I received the Grand Duke's instructions regarding yourself.
 MARY (*after a pause; angrily*) You know, there's a word for what *you* are, and it's not head of the Balkan Department.
 PETER. Miss Dagenham—I implore you not to leap to conclusions.
 MARY. I don't have to do any leaping to this conclusion. I can just walk straight there. (*She moves behind the desk towards the windows*) And I can walk straight out . . .
 PETER (*moving quickly to the upstage end of the desk*) But why this panic at a harmless little *tête à tête* supper?
 MARY. Listen. Where do you think I've been all my life? I know all about these harmless little *tête à tête* suppers. I've had to fight my way out of quite a few. "Champagne and I hope you like caviare and something cold to follow, because we really don't want the servants around, do we? It's so much more fun serving ourselves, don't you think?" And then after supper—"You must be tired after your show, Miss Dagenham, why don't you put your feet up on this nice sofa?" Oh, yes. I know every gambit. (*She turns away*)
 PETER. Aren't you confusing this legation with a private room at *Romano's*?

MARY. Well, where's the difference, except that here there's a longer run from the sofa to the door, and there's no evidence that Grand Dukes can't move just as fast as the next man? (*She moves below the desk*)

(PETER *moves down and intercepts Mary*)

No, seriously, I'm off. Make any excuse you like. My aunt's ill, or something.
PETER. Your aunt, Miss Dagenham?
MARY. I'm awfully sorry, really I am—but I just don't know why he should have to go and pick on me. I'm just about the only girl in the show who'd say no to a deal of this sort. I'm really funny that way—and get worried about myself, sometimes. Maybe I shouldn't be in musical comedy. It seems to give people the wrong ideas. Maybe I should have stuck to Shakespeare except that seemed to give people worse ones. Well, good-bye. (*She crosses between the supper table and the sofa towards the double doors*)
PETER (*moving quickly to* L *of the table and intercepting Mary; pleadingly*) Please, please, please. Do you want to get me and the whole Foreign Office into the most terrible trouble?
MARY. Since you ask, yes.
PETER (*coaxingly*) Now you don't mean that, Miss Dagenham. You know you don't. I'm sure you don't want to insult the Grand Duke, or to do the Entente a disservice. So why don't you just have a little supper with him? It'll be a very good one, and he's a most charming conversationalist. After supper—well—all you have to say is—"Well, good night, sir—it's been a most delightful evening, and now I must go home."
MARY. Yes—as an exit line that's swell, but can you personally guarantee the exit? This is a Balkan Grand Duke—for heaven's sake.
PETER. Educated at Eton.
MARY (*moving below the table*) That's what I mean. (*She crosses above the chair* LC *to the double doors*) No. I'm off.
PETER (*following Mary; frantically*) Wait a moment, please, please, Miss Dagenham. Supposing I do guarantee your exit, as you call it? Supposing I give you time for supper and then come in with a message from a hospital where your aunt has been taken after an accident . . .
MARY (*turning slightly; doubtfully*) Well—well—that's possible. Not more than half an hour, though.
PETER. But surely that isn't enough?
MARY (*with a step above the double doors*) It's far too much. After all don't . . .

(*The double doors are opened by the* FOOTMEN. PETER *steps back up* L *and bows. The* MAJOR-DOMO *backs in by the double doors and stands below the doorway.*)

His Royal Highness, The Grand Duke Charles, Prince Regent of Carpathia, *enters by the double doors. He is in evening dress with orders, and carries a brief-case.* Mary *freezes into silence. The* Regent *advances on Mary with outstretched hand*)

Regent (*taking Mary's hand*) How do you do?

(Mary *curtsies*)

So good of you to come at such short notice.

Mary. That's all right—Your Royal Highness.

Regent (*crossing below the supper table to the desk*) I must apologize for being late. (*He puts his brief-case on the desk*)

(Peter *moves up* c. *The* Major-Domo *takes Mary's cloak from her, moves to the door down* l *and exits.* Mary *follows the Major-Domo but stops behind the chair* lc)

The crowds are already gathering in the streets and my motor was held up. (*He turns to Peter*) Northbrook——

(Peter *moves up* r *of the table* c)

—I expect you're looking forward to your night's rest. We have a very full day before us.

Peter. We have indeed, sir.

Regent. The carriage leaves the legation for the Abbey at nine o'clock.

(*The* Major-Domo *enters down* l *and closes the door*)

If you are here at eight twenty?

Peter. Yes, sir.

Regent. Good night.

Peter. Good night, Your Royal Highness.

(Peter, *evidently conversant with the etiquette demanded at the Carpathian court, bows and backs skilfully to the double doors, where he bows again and exits.* Mary *moves to* l *of the supper table and watches Peter's manœuvre in awe and admiration*)

Regent (*to the Major-Domo*) Serve supper.

(*The* Major-Domo *bows, backs to the double doors and exits. The* Footmen *follow him off.* Mary *moves down a step or two and watches the Major-Domo depart*)

(*He moves down* rc) Were you surprised to get my invitation?

Mary (*turning*) I'll say I was. In fact I was so surprised I thought you couldn't possibly mean me.

Regent (*crossing to* r *of the chair* lc; *reassuringly*) But of course I meant you. I had your name most carefully marked down on my programme. In matters of this kind, I assure you, I am most methodical.

Mary. Oh. Yes. I can see you'd need to be.

REGENT. Who did you think I meant—if not you?
MARY. Well—Maisie Springfield.
REGENT. Oh, no. I have already met her, in Paris, some time ago.
MARY. I know. That's why I thought . . .
REGENT (*jovially*) Oh, no, no, no. Maisie Springfield. She is quite what I would call—old hat.
MARY. Oh. Would you? And I'm what you would call—new hat?
REGENT (*laughing politely*) Excellent, Miss—er—Miss——
MARY. You haven't got your programme handy?
REGENT (*laughing*) Capital. Most amusing.
MARY. Dagenham. Elaine Dagenham.

(*The* MAJOR-DOMO *enters by the double doors. He is followed on by the* BUTLER *and the two* FOOTMEN, *manœuvring a dumb waiter laid out with supper. The* BUTLER *crosses to* L *of the desk. The* MAJOR-DOMO *stands below the double doors. The* FOOTMEN *place the dumb waiter in the alcove up* C)

REGENT. Of course. How stupid of me.
MARY. That's just my stage name. My real name's Mary Morgan.
REGENT. You like caviare, I hope?
MARY (*resignedly*) Oh, yes.

(*The* FOOTMEN *pick up the caviare and butter, move* R *of the sofa and put the dishes on the supper table, which they move close to the sofa*)

REGENT (*moving to* L *of Mary*) I ordered a cold supper because then we can serve ourselves and that's so much more fun, don't you agree?
MARY (*resignedly*) Oh, yes. Much more fun.
REGENT (*moving above Mary to the supper table*) That is a charming dress.

(*The* FOOTMEN *cross and stand each side of the double doors*)

MARY. It's very old, I'm afraid.

(*The* REGENT *turns to the supper table and inspects the bottle of champagne.* MARY *makes a move to sit in the chair* LC, *but is stopped by a shocked hiss from the* MAJOR-DOMO, *and she moves below the supper table. The* REGENT *beckons to the* BUTLER, *who moves to the table, takes the bottle from the Regent, goes up* C *and opens the bottle*)

REGENT (*picking up the bottle of vodka*) Do you like vodka?
MARY. I've never tried it. I don't know whether . . .
REGENT (*filling two glasses with vodka*) Oh, you must. This is very special. (*He hands a glass to Mary*) Well, cheerioh! (*He throws his drink off at a gulp*)
MARY. Cheerioh! (*She sips her drink and makes a wry face*)

REGENT. No, no. Not to sip, like that. (*He refills his glass*) You will make yourself, as you say, tiddly. Like this—and then it has no dangerous effect. (*With the bottle in one hand and his glass in the other, he moves to* L *of* MARY *and again drinks off at a gulp*)

(MARY *closes her eyes and bravely gulps her drink. She stands quite still for a moment, with eyes closed, and then opens them in quiet amazement*)

MARY. I see what you mean.

(*The* REGENT *refills her glass*)

Oh no, no more, please.
REGENT. One more will not hurt a fly. (*He refills his glass*)
MARY. Possibly. But there's a saying about being as drunk as a fly, you know.

(*The* REGENT *laughs delightedly*)

REGENT. Oh, but that is really quite excellent. I can see you have a witty little tongue, Miss Dagenham.
MARY. Have I?
REGENT. Hurt a fly—drunk as a fly. I must remember that.
MARY. I really shouldn't bother, Your Royal Highness.
REGENT (*raising his glass*) Well—cheerioh!
MARY (*with some trepidation*) Cheerioh!

(*They both drink. This time* MARY *splutters. The* BUTLER *opens the champagne*)

REGENT. What's the matter?
MARY. That time I burnt my witty little tongue.
REGENT. Oh, that is very sad. (*He surveys her appraisingly, standing facing her*) I am quite delighted you're here, Miss—er—Dagenham. Quite delighted. I hope you are, too?

(*The* BUTLER *transfers the toast from the dumb waiter to the supper table*)

MARY. Oh, yes. Enraptured.
REGENT (*placing the bottle and his glass on the supper table*) Now will you sit here? (*He indicates the left end of the sofa*)

(*The* BUTLER *puts the bottle of champagne on the supper table, then moves the table out from the sofa to enable* MARY *to sit.* MARY *puts her glass on the supper table then sits on the sofa at the left end. The* BUTLER *pushes the table in to her, and moves up* LC. MARY *pushes the table out again as it is on her skirt, then pulls it to her. The* REGENT *signs to the* BUTLER, *who bows and backs out through the double doors. The* FOOTMEN *back out through the double doors, and are followed by the* MAJOR-DOMO *who backs out by the double doors and closes them.* MARY *watches them leave with regretful resignation, and watches the*

MAJOR-DOMO *back out, with a mixture of awe and trepidation, at the thought of having to do it herself*)

(*He pours two glasses of champagne*) Champagne? (*He hands a glass to Mary*)

MARY (*resignedly*) Yes.
REGENT. There, now we are to ourselves.
MARY (*resignedly*) Yes.

(*The* REGENT *holds out his glass to clink with* MARY's, *giving her what he plainly conceives to be a seductive smile.* MARY's *answering smile is resigned. They drink*)

REGENT (*briskly*) Good. Well, now, you will forgive me if I don't join you for the moment. I have already had dinner, and have one or two matters of business to attend to. (*Holding his glass he moves briskly to the desk, picks up his spectacles and puts them on, then takes a document from his brief-case and studies it*)

(MARY *looks extremely taken aback. Then she shrugs her shoulders and begins her supper, looking at her host between mouthfuls. The* REGENT *now appears completely oblivious of her. There is a long silence*)

MARY (*at length; brightly*) Turned quite warm all of a sudden, hasn't it? (*She takes off her gloves*)

(*The* REGENT *appears not to hear*)

(*She makes a little gesture of annoyance at herself. Muttering*) Wasn't addressed. (*She goes on with her food*)

(*The* REGENT *reaches out, picks up the telephone and lifts the receiver.* MARY *helps herself to caviare*)

REGENT (*into the telephone; in a low but perfectly audible voice*) Give me the Minister . . . Very well. Then wake him . . . Karnof? . . . Were you asleep? . . . I make no apologies. We are in the middle of a major crisis. I had an hour alone with Sir Edward and there is no question but that the arrest of Wolffstein has stirred up an international hornets' nest. I have an *aide-memoire* . . . What? . . . For heaven's sake, my dear fellow, don't talk Carpathian. You know I can't understand it properly . . . That's better . . . Yes, we can speak freely, there's no-one here . . . (*He perches himself on the downstage end of the desk*)

(MARY *slightly raises her eyebrows*)

I explained the entire situation to Sir Edward. I told him that if I hadn't had Wolffstein arrested there would have had to have been a general election. Wolffstein would certainly have come to power, and the French Alliance would have been revoked. Within a year we would have been allied to Germany, and Sir Edward did not need to be told that if that happened Wilhelm would at once force the issue with the Entente Powers on Morocco . . . Yes. Well, of course, he talked about the grave effect on public opinion, and I agree, it does not look too good to put the Leader of the Opposition in gaol on a charge of treason, but what else could I do? . . . Sir Edward requests that the trial be held in public, which makes it rather awkward.

(MARY *rises and, watching the Regent, moves to the dumb waiter*)

It means we shall have to get some evidence, and you know how difficult that is in these cases . . . Yes, he's a good man. I'll give him to Wolffstein as defending counsel. He'll certainly help us . . .

(MARY *puts some chicken salad on a plate, plainly listening to the conversation at the same time*)

But what has chiefly disturbed Sir Edward is the fact that those stupid Americans have protested . . .

(MARY, *on her way back to the supper table with her plate, stops short and glares at the Regent*)

Oh, some nonsense about political freedom, and democratic rights. You know what children the Americans are in matters of this kind. Their diplomacy always makes me think of the Minotaur Legend reversed—you know—the bull chasing Theseus through the labyrinth . . . Yes. A steam traction engine in Hampton Court maze. (*He chuckles*) Excellent . . .

(MARY *resumes her seat at the supper table and puts her plate down with an angry clatter. The* REGENT *looks up, rather absently smiles his seductive smile and raises his glass.* MARY's *answering smile is none too cordial, but the* REGENT *is far too preoccupied to notice*)

Oh, no. The British, of course, will be more sensible. They'll wait until *after* the trial, and then protest . . .

(MARY's *glance at the Regent is now ferocious*)

Yes, unhappily the American protest has been published in all our newspapers, and there have been a few riots tonight I hear . . . No. The situation is well under control, but oh, Herr Gott! When will those idiotic Americans grow up? . . . Yes. We will talk tomorrow. Good night. (*He replaces the receiver, puts down the telephone, sits for a moment deep in thought, and then appears to pull himself out of his reverie. He picks up his glass and strolls to* R *of the supper table. Heartily*) Well, well, well. And how is everything? (*He picks up the bottle of champagne*)

MARY (*glaring*) Just dandy.

REGENT. Ah, I see you have already served yourself. How remiss of me.

MARY. Oh, not at all. I prefer it that way.

REGENT. Splendid. (*He refills the two glasses, puts down the bottle and raises his glass*) Cheerioh! (*He drinks*)
MARY. Mud in your eye! (*She drinks*)

(*The* REGENT *splutters into his drink*)

REGENT. What a priceless expression! Wherever did you learn it?
MARY. In America.
REGENT (*absently*) Really? Have you been there?
MARY. I was born there. I *am* American.
REGENT (*looking at the telephone; deep in thought*) Are you, indeed?
MARY. Yes, Your Royal Highness.
REGENT. Will you excuse me? I've thought of another telephone call I must make.
MARY. Oh—that's quite all right. I just adore my own company.

(*The* REGENT, *with his glass in his hand, moves briskly to the telephone and lifts the receiver*)

REGENT (*into the telephone*) Connect me with the French Ambassador . . . Oh, yes, of course. He'll be at the reception. Well, I shall try later . . . (*He replaces the receiver, moves behind the desk, sits, puts on his spectacles and studies his document*)

(MARY *crossly pours herself some more champagne, then raises her glass*)

MARY (*firmly*) To President Taft.

(*There is no reply*)

I said—to President Taft.

(*Again there is no reply*)

(*She rises and drinks a lonely toast to her President. Muttering to herself*) O.K. So I wasn't addressed. So who cares? (*She resumes her seat*)

(*There is another silence*)

(*She rises with a sigh, moves to the dumb waiter and inspects the sweets. We can see that her various toasts have had a certain effect. Muttering to herself*) Bull in a labyrinth? Who the heck's Theseus, anyway? (*She helps herself to some trifle and resumes her seat on the sofa*)

(*The* REGENT *does not move, except occasionally to turn over a page*)

(*She mutters to herself*) Protest? I should darn well think they should protest. Arresting people like that. Disgraceful. (*She takes up the bottle. Still muttering*) Won't you have some more champagne, Miss Dagenham? (*She pauses*) Well, I don't know, Your Royal Highness. Do you really think I ought? (*She pauses*) Well, perhaps just a sip—(*she pours some champagne into her glass*) just up to there. Whoa! (*She puts down the bottle*)

REGENT (*looking up*) I beg your pardon? You said something?

MARY (*confused*) No, no. Just playing a little game over here—all by myself.

REGENT. Good. (*He raises his glass*) Cheerioh! (*He drinks*)

MARY (*raising her glass*) Chin, chin! (*She drinks*)

(*The double doors are suddenly imperiously thrown open.*

HIS MAJESTY KING NICOLAS THE EIGHTH OF CARPATHIA *enters by the double doors. He is a boy of about sixteen and wears a dressing-gown over pyjamas. He looks very grim. He takes in Mary quickly, and then turns to glare at the Regent*)

NICOLAS (*standing up* L) Why was I not informed of Wolffstein's arrest?

REGENT (*rising and moving up* C; *quietly*) Go back to bed, Nicky. We'll talk about it in the morning.

NICOLAS. No, Father. (*He closes the double doors*) We'll talk about it now. Why was I not informed of Wolffstein's arrest? Why was I left to learn it from the London *Evening Standard*?

REGENT (*patiently*) There was no need to inform you.

NICOLAS. No need to inform the King?

(MARY, *who, still tucking into the trifle, has been watching this exchange with interest, now rises quickly, knocking over a glass as she does so. Both* NICOLAS *and the* REGENT *glance at her*)

REGENT (*moving to* L *of the table* C; *perfunctorily*) May I present Miss Elaine Dagenham.

(MARY *moves above the chair* LC. NICOLAS *takes a step or two towards Mary and holds out his hand. The* REGENT *crosses above Nicolas and Mary and moves down* L)

NICOLAS (*equally perfunctory, but with royalty's well-trained smile*) Good evening.

(MARY *curtsies*)

(*He takes her hand*) It's delightful to meet you. Won't you sit down? (*He turns back to the Regent, switching the smile off with rapidity, leaving Mary in the curtsy position*) When the Leader of His Majesty's Opposition is thrown into prison on a trumped-up charge, His Majesty himself is apparently the last person to learn about it.

(MARY *rises from the curtsy position, philosophically shrugs her shoulders, resumes her seat on the sofa and returns to her trifle, her eyes on father and son*)

REGENT (*sitting in the chair down* L; *pacifically*) Your right to be informed I perfectly concede, Nicky, and it was only because your stepmother told me before she went out that you had gone to your bedroom with your Meccano set, and had left orders not to be disturbed, that I omitted to do so.

NICOLAS (*moving to* L *of the Regent*) That is mere evasion. By whose orders was Wolffstein arrested?

REGENT. By mine, of course.

NICOLAS. He must be released immediately.

REGENT (*quietly*) It seems to be my duty to point out to Your Majesty that it is only your right to information that I concede; not your right to give me orders. You have to wait another eighteen months for that.

NICOLAS (*moving down* LC) Oh? I wonder if you should count on that?

REGENT (*wearily*) I know exactly what that threat implies, Nicky, and so, I've no doubt, do my secret police.

NICOLAS. I don't understand what you mean by that. (*He moves to the chair* LC *and leans on it*) But it may happen that the people's anger at misgovernment, and at being dragged into a war on behalf of British imperialism and French greed, may perhaps take a drastic course—and sooner than you expect.

REGENT (*rising and crossing slowly down* R) Yes. You may be a real King very soon, Nicky, but for the moment I am still the ruler of Carpathia and of yourself. (*Sternly*) Go to your room.

(NICOLAS *stands undecided*)

Go to your room at once.

(NICOLAS *turns and moves slowly to the double doors*)

NICOLAS (*stopping and turning*) Where is Uncle Wilhelm now? At Potsdam?

REGENT. I don't know, but the Crown Prince is much more easily reached. He is staying at Buckingham Palace, and the number is Westminster eight-three-two.

(NICOLAS *turns abruptly to exit, then remembers his manners, turns and bows to* Mary)

NICOLAS (*with his royal smile*) Good night, Miss Dagenham. It has been a great pleasure.

MARY (*struggling to her feet*)—Good night, Your Majesty.

(NICOLAS *exits by the double doors, closing them behind him. The* REGENT *moves quickly to the telephone and lifts the reciver.* MARY *resumes her seat*)

REGENT (*into the telephone; quietly*) Colonel Hoffman . . . Hoffman—go to the King's bedroom, see if he's there, and lock him in. Better put a guard on as well. If he's not there, find him, wherever he is, and never leave him. Also—most important—put no telephone calls through to him—outward or inward until further notice. (*He replaces the receiver, sighs, stretches himself, then moves to* R *of the sofa*) It was most unfortunate that you should have been a witness to one of our little family quarrels. I'm so sorry to have embarrassed you.

MARY (*with wide eyes*) But he's your son, isn't he?

REGENT. Yes.

MARY. Your real son? Not a stepson, or anything?

REGENT. No.

MARY. Your only son?

REGENT. Yes.

MARY (*appalled*) Well!

(*There is a pause*)

Do you know—a moment ago I was good and mad at you . . .

REGENT. Good and mad? What is that expression?

MARY. It doesn't matter, because I'm not any more. Now I just feel terribly sorry for you. Oh, you poor, poor man.

REGENT (*sitting R of Mary on the sofa*) My dear Miss Dagenham, you really must not let Nicky's rather emotional tendencies mislead you too much. (*He refills their glasses*) He is merely expressing his loyalty to an old and long-established Carpathian royal tradition—that a son must of necessity oppose his father's policy. There was exactly the same tradition in English royal circles until quite recently.

MARY. But not plots—and secret police.

REGENT. Ah yes, but you see we're not a constitutional monarchy.

MARY (*with great firmness*) Ah. Now that's just the point. You should be.

REGENT (*politely*) You think so, Miss Dagenham?

MARY. I most certainly do think so. Putting people in prison for no reason, cooking up evidence—yes, I heard you—going against the popular will—it's all absolutely disgraceful, and if you want to know, I think the American State Department was absolutely right to protest. Incidentally, as I told you just now, only I don't think you heard me, I'm an American myself.

REGENT. Are you indeed, Miss Dagenham?

MARY. Yes, Your Royal Highness, that's what I am—an American citizen, and proud of it.

REGENT (*politely*) So you should be.

MARY. The Rights of Man—Government of the People—for the—(*the flow is interrupted by a slight hiccup*) and the rest of it. Oh, and *habeas corpus*—which is English really, but it's American, too . . .

REGENT. Yes. I have heard of it.

MARY (*severely*) And that means that you don't just go about arresting people because you don't agree with their political opinions. Poor Mr—what's his name—Wolffstein. (*She leans forward on the table*) He's probably got a wife—and a family—and—

oh, it's dreadful. I honestly don't know how you could do a thing like that. How could you?
  REGENT (*leaning forward on the table; quietly*) Because, in this case, I believe that the end justifies the means.
  MARY. Ah. Now, I could give an answer to that, if I'd had a little less to drink. (*She ponders a moment. Triumphantly*) I know. If the means are bad the end cannot be good. (*Surprised*) Who said that?
  REGENT. You did, I think.
  MARY. Did I? Imagine!
  REGENT. But in this case, you see, the end is world peace. Is that not an end good in itself?

  (*There is a pause*)

  MARY (*at length*) Difficult, isn't it?
  REGENT. Very.
  MARY. Look, I tell you. Why don't you just persuade this Mr Wolffstein to alter his policy?
  REGENT (*leaning back; smiling*) He is a very obstinate man, he is half German, and is in the pay of the Kaiser.
  MARY. Then get public opinion on your side.
  REGENT. A third of my people can't read or write and two-thirds are of German stock.

  (*There is a pause*)

  MARY. Yes.

  (*The* REGENT *reaches for the champagne bottle and picks it up*)

It really *is* tough—gosh!

  (*The telephone rings*)

  REGENT (*rising*) Excuse me. (*He crosses to the desk with the bottle and his glass*)
  MARY. Oh, darn it! Just when we were getting to be comfortable.

  (*The* REGENT *puts the bottle and glass on the desk and lifts the receiver*)

And I might have got a solution to the whole problem in a minute . . .
  REGENT (*into the telephone*) Yes? . . . I see. Very well. (*He replaces the receiver. Quietly*) My wife has come back from St James's Palace earlier than expected and is coming up for a moment.
  MARY. Oh. (*Suddenly realizing and jumping up*) Your wife! (*She moves to* L *of the sofa*) Oh, heavens! You'll want me to hide, then, won't you? Now where? (*She moves down* R *and points to the door down* R) In there? Or is there a cupboard?

REGENT (*quietly*) My dear—I see you have a very strong sense of the dramatic. I hate to disappoint you—but darting into cupboards—though it might be amusing for both of us—(*he goes to the sofa and picks up Mary's gloves*) is really not necessary. Besides—as always happens, I notice, on the stage—you'd be bound to leave something behind—like a glove or a fan—and we would both look foolish. (*He crosses to Mary and hands her the gloves*) No. just sit there—(*he pushes her gently into the chair down* R) and calm yourself. Now before you meet my wife I must warn you that she is a little vague and can be very deaf—on occasions . . .

(*The two* FOOTMEN *open the double doors.*

HER IMPERIAL AND ROYAL HIGHNESS, THE GRAND DUCHESS CHARLES *enters by the double doors. She is a woman of about the same age as the Regent, at the moment very resplendently dressed, having been at an official ball, beautiful and extremely regal. She is followed by a rather mousey-looking lady-in-waiting,* THE COUNTESS VON UND ZU MEISSENBRONN. *The* REGENT *crosses to the Grand Duchess. The* COUNTESS *stands just inside the doors, which are closed by the* FOOTMEN. *The* GRAND DUCHESS, *without glancing at the supper table or Mary, kisses the Regent on the cheek*)

GRAND DUCHESS. My dear! Such boredom! The decorations, hideous—and the music a catastrophe. (*She crosses to* LC) My carriage was ordered for one, but that strange little Turk drove us home—that one that May Herzogovina once lost her head about—do you remember? (*She moves to the sofa*)

(*The* REGENT *moves the table slightly to enable the* GRAND DUCHESS *to sit on the sofa, and waits for an interruption in the flow to present Mary*)

My dear, at dinner Olga Bosnia—who looked ridiculous, but I shall come back to that—had an accident with her ice—it was chocolate, I think, and it slid across the table into poor Rosie Schlumberger-Lippe-Gildenstern's lap—too killing—how we all roared—but that idiotic Olga laughed loudest of all and then had to say: "It was lucky it wasn't a *bombe surprise.*" Well—my dear, you can imagine! Such a silence you never heard. Afterwards she said she had quite forgotten that poor old Prince Schlumberger-Lippe-Gildenstern had been so brutally assassinated and anyway it wasn't a bomb, she said, it was a grenade, as if that made any difference. Now I must tell you how she was dressed . . . (*She breaks off*) Where is that idiotic Maud?

(*The* COUNTESS *moves behind the sofa*)

Oh, there you are, dear. I didn't see you. Give me a glass of that champagne—(*she points to the bottle on the desk*) I see over there.

SCENE I — THE SLEEPING PRINCE

(*The* COUNTESS *moves to the dumb waiter, collects a champagne glass, crosses to the desk and fills the glass with champagne*)

She had on a . . .
REGENT (*deftly interrupting*) My dear, might I present Miss Elaine Dagenham.

(*The* GRAND DUCHESS *extends a hand to* MARY, *who rises, come forward very nervously and takes the outstretched hand*)

GRAND DUCHESS (*with a gracious smile*) Ah yes, my dear, of course. I remember you well.
MARY. I'm quite sure you don't, Your Royal and—Your Imperial and Royal Highness.
GRAND DUCHESS (*to the Regent*) What does she say?
REGENT (*in a perfectly normal voice*) She says she is deeply flattered and compliments you on your wonderful memory.
GRAND DUCHESS (*to Mary*) Thank you, my dear.

(MARY *withdraws to make room for the* COUNTESS, *who puts the glass of champagne on the supper table near the Grand Duchess, then the* COUNTESS *crosses and stands* R *of the desk*)

(*To the Regent*) Sweetly pretty. She should use more mascara. When one is young one should use a *lot* of mascara and when one is old one should use much more. (*She sips the champagne, then helps herself to caviare*) Olga Bosnia—in baby pink, my dear, from head to foot. Ridiculous. She looked like one of those revolting cakes that one gets when one has tea with dear Irene Besserabia—and which she says melt in one's mouth and in fact squirt all over the palace. Tiara—over one eye, and false, of course—as we all know —incidentally May Herzogovina says she bought the original in a pawnshop in Salonika and that that was false, too—but May is not strictly truthful, I'm afraid. (*She turns abruptly to Mary*) And what do you do, my dear?
MARY. I'm in *The Coconut Girl* at *The Gaiety*.

(*The* GRAND DUCHESS *sips her champagne and looks enquiringly at the Regent*)

GRAND DUCHESS. Yes?
REGENT. She says she is an actress.
GRAND DUCHESS. An actress? How interesting. Madame Bernhardt has stayed with us, you know. Personally I do not find her so good in *Magda* as Mademoiselle Duse. You agree, no?
MARY (*baffled*) No.
GRAND DUCHESS. You don't agree? That is interesting. You know Lucien Guitry, too?
MARY. No, ma'am.
GRAND DUCHESS. Only Madame Bernhardt. You are quite right to be loyal to your friends, my dear. Loyalty is a quality

that we do not see enough nowadays. *Très bien.* (*She pats Mary's lap with her fan*) I saw her in *Phèdre* not long ago. You, of course, must have seen her countless times—so close to her as you are—*mais ma chère—entre nous*—I found the play quite irritating—so much love—most tedious. I never know why people want to write about love when there are so many more pleasant subjects to choose from. (*She rises. To the Regent*) Well, my dear, I must go to bed.

(*The* REGENT *pulls the table forward a little*)

(*She moves below the table*) Which uniform are you wearing to-morrow?

REGENT. Royal Guards.

GRAND DUCHESS. Now let me see—what colour? (*After a thought*) Yes, that's all right. We won't clash. Good night, my dear.

REGENT. Good night, my dear.

(*The* GRAND DUCHESS *and the* REGENT *kiss each other on the cheek, then the* REGENT *moves to the double doors, knocks on them, and returns to* LC)

GRAND DUCHESS (*moving* LC) Maud! Where is that idio——

COUNTESS (*moving above the sofa*) Here, ma'am.

(*The* FOOTMEN *open the double doors*)

GRAND DUCHESS. Oh, yes. Run ahead, dear, and find my book.

(*The* COUNTESS *crosses to the double doors*)

You know what it is, don't you. *The Life and Trial of Doctor Crippen.* I shall want you to read to me for twenty minutes . . .

COUNTESS (*with a curtsy*) Yes, ma'am.

GRAND DUCHESS. Maud—you look very pinched. What is the matter with you?

COUNTESS. I have a slight cold.

GRAND DUCHESS (*solicitously*) Oh, poor thing! I'm so very, very sorry. I must make you one of my syrups.

COUNTESS. So kind of you, ma'am.

(*From her expression we see the* COUNTESS *has experienced one of the Grand Duchess's syrups before. She curtsies and backs out by the double doors. The* GRAND DUCHESS, *with the gracious smile hardly off her face, moves up* R *of the Regent*)

GRAND DUCHESS. Idiotic creature, always catching cold. I really can't think how. As far as I know, her life is quite blameless. Anyway—with a face like that . . . (*She turns graciously to Mary*) Good night, my dear. So delightful——

MARY. Good night, ma'am.

GRAND DUCHESS. —and just a touch more on the cheeks, too, I think.

MARY. Yes, ma'am.

(*The* GRAND DUCHESS *smiles her farewell and goes to the double doors, where she turns, looking severe*)

GRAND DUCHESS. Don't make mischief between me and Madame Bernhardt, now—or I shall be cross.

(*The* GRAND DUCHESS *exits. The* FOOTMEN *close the double doors*)

MARY (*crossing to* R *of the table* C) A *little* vague? Well! Say, listen—didn't she mind *at all* about you and me?

(*There is a pause. The* REGENT *moves to* L *of the table* C, *takes a cigarette from the box on it*)

REGENT (*slowly*) My dear, I proposed to my wife because I needed to reinforce the Austrian Trade agreement. She accepted me because the Emperor told her to. For ten years we have been utterly and completely devoted to each other, with never a single unkind word spoken on either side. Why should she *mind*?

(*There is a pause*)

MARY (*at length*) I think it's dreadful.
REGENT (*puzzled*) Something else is dreadful?
MARY. I find your life quite shocking—and you know why?
REGENT (*striking a match*) Why? (*He lights his cigarette*)
MARY. Because there's no love in it.

(*The* REGENT *opens his mouth to reply*)

(*Interrupting; scornfully*) Oh, yes. Maisie Springfields by the bushel load, I've no doubt. I meant, real *love*.

(*The telephone rings*)

(*Angrily*) Oh. Not again!
REGENT (*crossing to the telephone*) Excuse me. (*He lifts the receiver and sits behind the desk. Into the telephone*) Yes . . . (*Gravely*) I see . . . How many casualties? . . . Not so serious, then . . .

(MARY *moves to the chair* LC *and sits*)

My dear fellow, there's no need to panic. But the new Chief of Police is a good man and I trust him . . . No. (*He replaces the receiver, looking distracted*)

(MARY *closely watches the* REGENT, *who comes out of his reverie and catches her eye. He smiles his automatic seductive smile, as he does so surreptitiously looking at his watch*)

(*Heartily*) Well, my dear. (*He rises and crosses to Mary*)
MARY. Well.
REGENT. My dear, wouldn't you be more comfortable on the sofa? You could put your feet up there and rest.

MARY (*after a pause*) I think I'll stay here, thank you.
REGENT. Very well. Just as you please. (*He moves to the chair down* L, *sits and studies* MARY *as she sits in the chair, evidently calculating possible lines of attack. He kicks the footstool to* MARY'S *chair, then rises, and sits on the footstool, putting his arm around* MARY'S *waist*)

(*There is a pause*)

My dear—it was so good of you to come and see me tonight.
MARY (*her voice at a rather nervous pitch*) You said that before.
REGENT. Did I? (*The posture now seems rather cramped for him and he plainly suffers from a momentary twinge of rheumatism, for he withdraws his hand and twitches his shoulders with an expression of discomfort. Then he methodically places the stool in a more convenient position and lays his hand once more on her waist*) That is a beautiful dress.
MARY. You said that before too.
REGENT (*amorously*) What does it matter? What are words—what are words, where deeds can say so much more? (*This is plainly his accustomed cue for action. With a fairly practised, if not exactly lissom swing, he heaves himself, with just the faintest giving at the knees, on to the arm of the chair. He bends his head forward tenderly for the embrace*)

(MARY *jabs the* REGENT *hard in the stomach with her elbow*)

MARY. Say that's just terrible. (*She pushes him aside with her arm, rises and crosses to* R *of the supper table*)
REGENT (*holding his stomach*) What is terrible?
MARY. That performance of yours.
REGENT (*rising; aggrieved*) I fear I do not altogether understand you, Miss Dagenham.
MARY. Now, don't come the Grand Duke on me. There's no need for that. You made a pass. I turned it down. That's all that's happened. We can still be friendly.

(*There is a pause, then the* REGENT *moves abruptly to the supper table*)

REGENT. Excuse me. (*He picks up the vodka bottle and pours himself a drink, throwing it straight back*)
MARY. Say—listen—I could do with a small one, too.

(*The* REGENT *moves below the supper table and fills* MARY'S *glass*)

(*She picks up her glass*) I need it for my heart. It's still pounding away down here . . .
REGENT (*stiffly*) I'm so sorry.
MARY. Oh, it's not your fault. In fact if I'd known that that was all that was going to happen, I wouldn't have been nervous at all. (*She raises her glass*) Well—long life and good health to Your Royal Highness.
REGENT (*automatically*) Cheerioh!

MARY (*naughtily*) And better luck next time. (*She drains her glass with a gulp and replaces it on the table*) Say—there *is* something to that stuff, you know. Sure it has no effect—drunk that way?

REGENT. After three of them, you might experience a certain euphoria. (*He takes the bottle of vodka and puts it on the dumb waiter*) I think you have had enough.

MARY (*moving above the sofa*) O.K. I admit I *was* feeling a bit muzzy a moment ago, but your rendition of the balcony scene, just now, sobered me up.

(*There is a pause. The* REGENT *looks impatiently at his watch*)

REGENT. How is your heart, now?

MARY. Fine. Right back to normal. I'll tell you why I was so nervous, Your Royal Highness. You see—I thought I was going to have a real struggle with myself tonight. I should have explained to you early on that I don't do this sort of thing as a rule, you know, on account of I'm a well-known eccentric—and that's what I usually do explain right at the beginning of supper, because I think it's fair—but this time we didn't seem to have much chit chat together before the curtain went up and so I never somehow got the cue. So then when it did go up I thought, here we go, girl—this is it. He's a Grand Duke with Balkan fire in his veins, and there's going to be a flood of turgid intoxicating love talk. And then I thought—well—the court musicians will be playing Tzigane music just outside the door, and the lights will be discreetly dimmed, and there will be a strange seductive perfume in the air—and well—I just thought, well, you'd better watch out, girl, I thought. You'd just better watch out. (*With a sigh*) Oh well! (*She yawns, stretches herself and leans on the back of the sofa. Interestedly*) Tell me, do they all fall as easily as that—the Maisies and the others?

REGENT (*with controlled anger*) Before your insults grow too great to be borne, Miss Dagenham, I am ringing for your car. (*He moves to the table* C *and rings the bell*)

MARY. O.K. That's a deal, except I haven't got a car.

REGENT (*moving up* C; *angrily*) A cab, then.

MARY. Sure—but—I live way out in Brixton.

REGENT (*moving to the table* L) I shall naturally arrange for you to be escorted to your home.

MARY. I can do the tip. (*She moves to* L *of the table* C)

(*The* REGENT *picks up a magazine from the table* L)

Er—I guess I'll get my wrap then.

(*The* REGENT *tosses the magazine on to the table* L, *moves to the door down* L *and opens it, then strides across to* R)

(*She crosses to the door down* L) Thank you. (*She appears to remember something and stops*) Oh, sorry. (*She turns round and proceeds to walk gingerly backwards through the door. Triumphantly, having reached her objective*) Pretty good, huh?

(MARY *exits and closes the door. The* REGENT *stands for a moment, scowling.*
The MAJOR-DOMO *enters by the double doors and bows*)

REGENT (*savagely*) Why am I deserted? Why is there no-one to answer a bell?

MAJOR-DOMO (*coming forward a couple of steps*) With respect, Your Royal Highness yourself gave orders that the attendants were to be moved from the door.

REGENT (*moving up* RC) See that a taxi is fetched at once, and tell the A.D.C. on duty he is to escort Miss Dagenham to a place called Brixton.

MAJOR-DOMO. As your Royal Highness commands. (*He bows and begins to back out*)

REGENT (*looking at his watch*) Wait.

(*The* MAJOR-DOMO *stops*)

One of my personal servants plays the violin. Who is that?

MAJOR-DOMO. I think it is Franz, Your Royal Highness—one of the under valets.

REGENT. Does he play it well?

MAJOR-DOMO. I am tone deaf, Your Royal Highness.

REGENT. Where is he now?

MAJOR-DOMO. In bed, sir.

REGENT (*moving down* RC) Fetch him out of it. Tell him I may need him to play his confounded fiddle outside this door. (*He indicates the supper table*) And take this away.

(*The* REGENT *crosses to the door down* R *and exits. The* MAJOR-DOMO *crosses to the supper table and whisks it above the chair* LC.
The REGENT *re-enters. He carries a scent spray and sprays all around the room*)

Wait.

(*The* MAJOR-DOMO *stops and turns*)

Not directly outside the door. That would seem too obvious. Let me see, now. About ten paces down the passage . . .

MAJOR-DOMO (*nodding*) Just outside the Minister's bedroom?

REGENT (*crossing to the switches up* L) Yes. Station him there at once. (*He switches off the wall-bracket lights*) But don't let him begin until I ring. (*He switches off the chandelier*) I will probably not need him at all. (*He moves to the table down* L *and switches off the table-lamp then crosses down* R)

MAJOR-DOMO (*pushing the supper table to the double doors*) And the taxi—Your Royal Highness?

(*The* 1st Footman *takes the supper table from the Major-Domo and exits with it*)

Regent (*angrily*) Use your own judgement.

(*The* Major-Domo *bows low and backs out through the double doors, closing them as he goes.*
The Regent *exits down* R *and re-enters immediately, without the scent spray. He closes the door and moves to the table up* R *to switch out the light. Before he can do so,* Mary *enters down* L*, closing the door behind her*)

Mary. Say—Your Royal Highness—that's some bedroom you've got in there. Yours?
Regent. No. It's the room they prepared for the Grand Duchess, but she prefers a room on the garden side.
Mary. I see. Well—this is my exit, I guess.

(*The* Regent *crosses to the double doors, then stops and turns.* Mary *follows the Regent and holds out her hand. The* Regent *tenderly takes her hand.* Mary *is going into her curtsy, but the* Regent *lifts her gently up*)

Regent. Please. This is not, quite yet, good-bye. (*He leads her down* C) Give me just one minute to tell you how deeply distressed I feel at what has happened between us.
Mary (*murmuring*) Listen—I'm the one that should be sorry . . .
Regent (*pleadingly*) Please, please. Let me try and explain a little about something that is in my mind at the moment. Won't you sit down—just for a second?
Mary (*moving to the sofa*) The taxi isn't ticking up, is it?
Regent (*moving to* L *of Mary*) No. They will tell us when it arrives.

(Mary *sits on the edge of the sofa*)

It is simply this, my dear. I have behaved to you tonight like a cad and a boor and you must accept my most heartfelt apologies. (*He moves down* R) But in my defence let me say this—I have many things to disturb me at this moment—you know some of them. (*He moves to the table* R) And just now I learnt that there are terrible riots tonight all over my country—tomorrow I may have to declare martial law. (*He switches out the lamp on the table* R) And —well—(*he crosses to the table* C) You remember what Shakespeare said, "It is hard to sleep well with a crown on your head." (*He moves to the dumb waiter and pours a glass of vodka*)
Mary. Not quite that, but the meaning's clear.
Regent. I am so bitterly, my dear, so heartbrokenly unhappy that you should leave me now, at my darkest hour, with harsh, cruel hating thoughts. I am a very lonely person . . . (*He approaches Mary with the glass of vodka*)

(MARY *absently takes the glass*)

You cannot possibly understand, with your happy childish soul, what it would mean to me if I could only find someone like yourself to share my life. (*He glances surreptitiously at his watch*) If only I hadn't spoiled everything just now. Ah, what fools these human beings be.

MARY (*murmuring*) Mortals. (*She absently throws the drink back*) Hey! I didn't ask for that.

REGENT (*taking the glass from Mary*) You are right about my life. (*He puts the glass on the table* C *then moves to* L *of the sofa*) It is quite without love. I am growing into middle age . . .

MARY. Oh, no . . .

REGENT. Almost into middle age. My life has fallen into the sere and yellow leaf.

MARY (*mildly surprised*) Well, now! You got that one right.

REGENT. Yes. Here am I, having reached the age of fort—— thirty nine—and I have never known what it is to love or be loved. It is like the legend of the Sleeping Princess. (*He leans over the left end of the sofa*) Only here it is the Prince that sleeps—and awaits the kiss of the beautiful young maiden that will bring him back to life.

(*There is a pause*)

MARY (*at length*) You mean you want me to kiss you?

REGENT (*moving above the sofa*) You are so literal. (*With a deep sigh*) It is love that I need. The ennobling love of a pure young woman—her bright faith in me as I am and as I might yet be— her glowing self-sacrifice to my little weaknesses and desires—for love is sacrifice, is it not?

(MARY *settles on her left side into the left corner of the sofa, with her feet still on the floor, but relaxed and apparently content, her eyes half closed*)

Yes. There is the mystic kiss that might bring this sleeping Prince to life. (*He pauses, having plainly been embarrassing himself with this dialogue. He looks at Mary to see how it has been going down*)

MARY (*at length; noticing the pause*) O.K. I got you.

REGENT (*leaning over the back of the sofa*) Do you know what your hair reminds me of? (*He reaches out, unseen by Mary, and rings the bell on the table* C) Summer corn, kissed by the wind into enchantingly exciting furrows.

(*A violin, playing a Tzigane melody, can be heard off*)

Your eyes . . . (*He breaks off, listens and nods approvingly*)

MARY. Say—where's that music coming from? (*She sits up*)

REGENT. One of my servants, a Hungarian, always plays at this hour. He is lamenting his lost love.

MARY (*disturbed*) Oh, poor darling. (*She raises herself a little* then leans back, puts her head on the right end of the sofa, and puts her feet up on the left end. With a deep sigh) Oh, isn't life awful? (*Evidently rising above the awfulness of life*) You were saying about my eyes . . . ?

REGENT (*moving to* R *of the sofa*) Twin pools—of gladness and joy—in which any man would be glad to drown himself. (*He leans over above Mary's face*)

MARY (*sleepily*) You mean—in both?

REGENT (*a shade crossly*) In either.

MARY. Anyway, I like twin pools. That's good. Twin pools. Go on.

REGENT (*straightening up*) Your chin . . . (*He comes round in front of the sofa and looks at Mary*)

MARY. You left out my nose.

REGENT (*seating himself on the edge of the sofa*) Of course. What can one say of perfection?

MARY (*dreamily*) That's O.K. Now go back to my chin.

REGENT. This is what I think of your chin. (*Far more expertly than the last time, his position, of course, is easier for him, he kisses her chin*)

(MARY *does not resist. The* REGENT *kisses* MARY's *mouth, and she responds*)

My darling—oh, my darling!

MARY (*emerging from the embrace*) That poor Hungarian! Oh, I do hope he gets his love back. (*She keeps time sleepily with her hand*)

REGENT. Don't think of *his* love. Think of ours. (*He kisses her*)

MARY (*fingering his hair-dreamily*) Gosh! Your hair's pretty.

REGENT (*tenderly*) Do you think so?

MARY. You put the wrong stuff on it, though. What do you use?

REGENT. A little pomade.

MARY. Now, that's where you're wrong.

REGENT. Darling . . .

MARY. You should use——

REGENT. I shall remember.

MARY. —Pinaud's lilac.

REGENT (*a shade impatiently*) I asked you, my darling, to remember our love . . .

MARY (*dreamily*) Your eyebrows are pretty, too.

REGENT (*interrupting imperiously*) Love! What a universe of joy and pain lies in that little word!

(*There is a pause while* MARY *stares thoughtfully at the face so close to hers. The Tzigane music seems to come closer. It is certainly louder. One wonders if the Major-Domo has his eye to the keyhole*)

MARY (*suddenly*) All right. *You* asked for it. (*She draws his head down and gives him a prolonged passionate kiss*)

(*There is a discreet knock at the door, unnoticed. Then one less discreet. Finally, an agitated-looking* PETER *enters by the double doors. The embrace continues.* PETER *coughs. The* REGENT *jumps to his feet and moves quickly to* R *of the sofa*)

PETER. If Your Royal Highness—will forgive this intrusion . . .
REGENT (*furiously*) This is intolerable!
PETER (*moving down* L) With deepest respect, sir, my message is so important that I had no choice but to intrude.
REGENT. Revolution?
PETER. No, sir. Miss Dagenham's aunt has been in a motor accident.
MARY (*half rising*) What? (*She turns her head and looks at Peter, and remembrance comes back*) Oh, go away, you silly man!
PETER (*with a step towards Mary*) But your aunt—Miss Dagenham—you realize how very serious her condition . . .
MARY. It's her own fault. She's no right to be out in an automobile as late as this, at ninety three . . .
PETER (*protestingly*) But, Miss Dagenham . . .
REGENT (*roaring*) Miss Dagenham asked you to go away—and I *command* you to go away.
PETER (*backing towards the double doors*) Your Royal Highness . . .
REGENT (*crossing below the sofa*) I am most seriously displeased at this breach of etiquette, Mr Northbrook, and shall no doubt find opportunity of expressing my displeasure in certain quarters.
PETER. Your Royal Highness . . .
REGENT. Go.

(PETER *disappears hastily backwards through the double doors, closing them as he goes.* MARY, *from the sofa, makes a carefree gesture of dismissal. The* REGENT *moves to* L *of Mary and raises her*)

REGENT (*with a wide gesture*) Come, my darling.
MARY. Where to? (*After thinking it out*) Oh. I know what you mean. (*She swings her legs round to a sitting position*) I've got euphoria like mad. (*Still sitting, she looks up, a little hazily, at the Regent*)

(*The* REGENT *still holds his amorous gesture and seductive expression*)

(*Sharply*) Listen, before I go one step further, I must utter a solemn warning.
REGENT. Utter it, my beloved.
MARY. If I *do* go one step further, you know what's going to happen? I'm going to fall in love with you. I always, always do.
REGENT (*gently*) Always?
MARY. Both times. (*Darkly*) So you just watch out, that's all. You just watch out.

REGENT. But why? Isn't your loving me exactly what I crave for?
MARY. Not unless you're even crazier than you look—swaying about there——

(*The* REGENT *crosses to* R *of Mary*)

—with that star thing twinkling all over the place and your hair all mussed.
REGENT (*resuming the gesture*) Come, my dear.
MARY. One step further?
REGENT (*imperiously*) Come with me.
MARY (*sighing*) You poor man. You poor, poor man.

(*The* REGENT *crosses to the door down* R *and opens it*)

All right. You're for it, then. All right. (*She rises with difficulty*) One step further. (*She takes it, with catastrophic results. Her knees seem quietly to collapse under her, and with a resigned sigh, she crumples slowly to the floor, ending, at length, in a comfortable position on her back, staring at the ceiling*) Oh. What lovely cherubs on the ceiling.

(*The* REGENT *moves to Mary and bends over her*)

(*She gathers her cloak around her*) Good night, my darling. Good night. See you in the morning. (*She turns over into a dormant position*)

(*The* REGENT *strides angrily to the table* C, *rings the bell then moves up* C.
The MAJOR-DOMO *enters immediately by the double doors. The* REGENT *nods in the direction of the recumbent Mary. The* MAJOR-DOMO *goes over, his face impassive, and looks down at her, then nods enquiringly at the door down* L. *The* REGENT *shrugs his shoulders impatiently. The* MAJOR-DOMO *signals towards the double doors.*
The BUTLER *and the two* FOOTMEN *enter. The Tzigane melody is continuing*)

REGENT (*shouting*) Stop that infernal din!

(*The music ceases. The* MAJOR-DOMO *collects Mary's gloves and handbag. The* BUTLER *and the two* FOOTMEN *cross to Mary. The* MAJOR-DOMO *crosses and opens the door down* L. *The* BUTLER *and the two* FOOTMEN *pick Mary up*)

(*He crosses to the door down* R) Herr Gott noch mal! How do you expect a man to get any sleep?

The REGENT *exits down* R, *angrily slamming the door. The* BUTLER *and the* FOOTMEN *carry Mary towards the door down* L *as—*

the CURTAIN *falls*

Scene 2

SCENE—*The same. Eight-thirty the following morning.*

When the CURTAIN *rises, the* MAJOR-DOMO *is standing* L *of the desk supervising the preparation of the breakfast table by the* BUTLER *and the* 1ST FOOTMAN. *The* 1ST FOOTMAN *holds a tray with cups and coffee, etc. for two.* PETER *enters by the double doors. He is in full dress diplomatic uniform. The* BUTLER *and the* 1ST FOOTMAN, *with his tray, retire up* C *and during the ensuing episode, stand, rock-like, staring impassively ahead. The* MAJOR-DOMO *greets Peter with a bow, and then, out of sight of the Butler and Footman, makes a slight movement, indicating his wish to speak with him.* PETER *crosses to the* MAJOR-DOMO *who moves down* R. *They circle anti-clockwise and begin a whispered colloquy, of which no sound is ever audible, but the purport is fairly plain owing to the number of glances both of them continually make towards the door down* L. PETER'S *face is grave and deeply disturbed; the* MAJOR-DOMO'S *impassive. At length,* PETER *nods, and goes hesitantly to the door down* L. PETER *knocks gently on the door. Then again, less gently. Finally, after an exchange of glances with the* MAJOR-DOMO, *he opens the door and looks into the room. He closes the door immediately and nods to the Major-Domo. The inaudible colloquy begins again.* PETER *moves to* R *of the* MAJOR-DOMO *and they circle again, this time, clockwise.*

PETER (*at length*) I'd better go and ask. (*He crosses to the door down* R *and knocks on it*)

REGENT (*off; calling*) Yes? Who?

PETER (*calling*) Northbrook, sir.

REGENT (*off; calling*) Come in.

(PETER *exits down* R, *leaving the door ajar, and we hear the murmur of his discreetly lowered voice, followed by a sudden short, enraged bellow from the* REGENT. PETER *re-enters hastily backwards, and closes the door*)

PETER (*harassed*) One place. (*He goes to the window and gazes out*)

(*The* MAJOR-DOMO *nods, makes the necessary signal to the Butler and Footman, then stands* L *of the desk and gazes past Peter, out of the window. The* BUTLER *and* FOOTMAN *move to the table* C, *set out coffee for one, then exit by the double doors, closing them as they go. As the double doors close,* MARY *enters down* L, *blinking in the daylight. Her hair is tousled, and she is swathed in a large bed-cover, on which the royal arms of Carpathia are boldly displayed. Unseen by either Peter or the Major-Domo, she goes slowly towards the table* C, *walking rather as if every step she takes is jarring a very tender head, and pours herself a glass of iced water, which she drinks in a single gulp. She bangs the glass down.* PETER *and the* MAJOR-DOMO *turn*)

SCENE 2   THE SLEEPING PRINCE

(*He crosses below the desk*) Miss Dagenham—I must have a word with you, please.

(MARY *gives a faint croak, picks up the water carafe and glass from the table, turns, moves to the door down* L *as gingerly as she had come and exits.* PETER *turns to the Major-Domo and enquiringly raises his eyebrows. The* MAJOR-DOMO *almost imperceptibly shrugs his shoulders. All the* MAJOR-DOMO'S *gestures are almost imperceptible. He crosses to the door down* L*, closes it, then moves to the double doors.* PETER *hovers behind the sofa, looking worried. The* MAJOR-DOMO *opens the double doors, then steps backwards and bows.*

NICOLAS *enters by the double doors. He is dressed in a plain blue suit.* PETER, *on seeing Nicolas, bows*)

NICOLAS. Good morning, Mr Northbrook.

(*The* MAJOR-DOMO *exits by the double doors, closing them as he goes*)

PETER. Good morning, sir.

NICOLAS (*moving below the sofa*) My father has sent for me. Am I to go in?

PETER. I think, perhaps, better not, sir. His valets are with him, and he is having a little trouble with his top boots. He should be out in a moment.

(NICOLAS *throws himself on to the sofa, and picks up a morning newspaper from the left arm*)

NICOLAS (*looking at the paper; impatiently*) Coronation. Coronation. Coronation. Nothing about the rest of the world. Nothing about my own country, where there is practically civil war.

PETER (*moving to* R *of the sofa*) You are surely exaggerating, sir. I understand the situation in Carpathia is well under control.

NICOLAS (*muttering*) The wrong control. That's the trouble. (*He looks up at Peter*) Yes. Report that remark to the Foreign Office. I don't care.

PETER. Your Majesty does me an injustice.

NICOLAS. Only in the sense that you would be reporting nothing that they did not know already.

PETER (*moving above the desk; chattily*) Splendid weather for the Coronation, isn't it, sir? I understand you are seeing the procession from a window in the *Ritz Hotel*. You should have an exceptionally good view. A pity that you cannot go to the Abbey, but, of course, protocol forbids it. Who is accompanying your Majesty?

NICOLAS. My gaoler, of course.

PETER. Your gaoler, sir?

NICOLAS. Colonel Hoffman.

(PETER *smiles mirthlessly and moves to the window.*

The REGENT *enters down* R*, closing the door behind him. He is wearing a dressing-gown, under which we see top boots*)

REGENT (*crossing above the sofa to* L *of the table* C) Nicky, I trust you have not forgotten that you are entertaining your Aunt Maria and Cousin Louisa at seven this evening?

NICOLAS (*gloomily*) No, Father.

REGENT. And as you won't be seeing your little cousin again for some time, and as we will probably want to make an official announcement soon, it might be as well if you gave her some slight indication of your feelings for her.

NICOLAS (*boldly*) May the indication be as slight as the feelings?

REGENT (*pouring a cup of coffee for himself; sharply*) Nicky! Don't be ridiculous! You know you find little Louisa very attractive. You told me so yourself.

NICOLAS. I said I liked the way she looked when she was skating, that's all. Is that such a strong basis for marriage? I mean, what do I do in the summer? Anyway, I find her most unintelligent and snobbish.

REGENT. Nonsense! You're devoted to her, and she to you. It's only that you're sulking because of Wolffstein's arrest.

NICOLAS. That issue is far too important for mere sulking, Father. You have granted me my right to information. What has happened in my country since last night?

REGENT. The riots are still continuing. As they appear to be well organized—(*he watches Nicky as he crosses behind the sofa to* R *of it*) I have had no option but to order certain further arrests.

NICOLAS (*sharply*) Further arrests?

REGENT. I have the list on me, I think. (*He takes out a piece of paper from his dressing-gown pocket*) Yes. Here it is . . .

(NICOLAS *snatches the paper and hastily runs his eye down it*)

Any friends of yours there?

NICOLAS (*blandly*) I am not allowed to have politicians for friends, Father. You know that. (*He hands the list back,* plainly rather relieved, rises, moves to the double doors and opens the upstage half)

REGENT (*pacifically*) Nicky, I have arranged for Harrods to send you a new Meccano set.

NICOLAS (*turning eagerly*) What number?

REGENT. Number four.

NICOLAS (*with a childish wail*) Oh, but I've got number four. It's number five I want. Oh, Father—really!

(NICOLAS *exits, closing the door behind him. The* REGENT *wheels in front of the desk and rounds on Peter*)

REGENT (*explosively*) That idiot Hoffman! He swore it was number four. The consequences of such a blunder could be serious.

PETER. I shall see that the mistake is rectified immediately, sir.

(*The* REGENT *moves above the table* C)

SCENE 2 — THE SLEEPING PRINCE

REGENT (*nodding and scrutinizing his list of ringleaders*) Now I wonder who it is I've left off this list? There was some name he was looking for, and was relieved to find not there. (*He studies the list for a moment, with a puzzled frown. At length*) Verflucht! (*He puts the list in his pocket, picks up his cup of coffee, then crosses above the sofa to* L *of Peter*) Well? You have got rid of her?

PETER (*crossing to* R *of the sofa*) Er—not yet, sir. There has been so little time.

REGENT (*alarmed*) You mean she is still there?

(PETER *nods*)

She might come out at any moment?

PETER. She has already been out.

REGENT (*muttering*) Is there a lock on this side of the door?

(PETER *crosses to the door down* L *and examines the lock*)

PETER. I'm afraid not.

REGENT (*crossing and sitting in the chair* LC) Um Gottes Willen! (*He hastily gulps his coffee*)

PETER (*diffidently*) Do I gather, sir, that the evening was not an unqualified success?

REGENT (*looking ferociously at Peter*) Northbrook, this Foreign Office parlance of yours, I begin to find irritating. (*Fiercely*) The evening was an unqualified nightmare.

PETER (*crossing above the chair* LC *and below the sofa to* R *of it*) Oh, I'm so sorry, sir. What went wrong?

REGENT (*angrily*) Everything went wrong—but chiefly the girl.

PETER (*with a snigger*) I thought the trouble was rather the reverse.

REGENT. That is not humorous. This is not a humorous matter, Northbrook. I have only one evening, in London, one single evening, in which I can hope to arrange for myself a little—relaxation. And what happens? Out of the whole of this vast teeming city—teeming with beautiful willing women—the most beautiful, if not always the most willing on earth—you find me what? A little American ninnycompoop.

PETER. With respect, sir—either ninny by itself or nincompoop.

REGENT. Ninnycompoop will serve. She fully deserves a new word. The mind of a backward child, the muscles of a boxer and an approach to life of such stomach-turning sentimentality that I found myself, Northbrook, I found myself last night, uttering phrases which—had any single one of them been overheard—would have made me the laughing-stock of Europe. And—to crown it all—and at the crucial moment—she is rendered insensible by an amount of vodka which, in Carpathia, you would add to the bread and milk of a four-year-old, as a mild tonic. I am not pleased with your part in the affair, Northbrook. I am distinctly not pleased.

PETER. But, again, with respect, sir, my part in the affair was limited to carrying out your orders.

REGENT (*pointing an accusing finger*) And who was it who said to me, "Why do you not invite this little actress to supper?" Who?

PETER. Ah. But it was your initial interest in the lady, sir, that inspired me to that remark. I was not to know how unsuitable a guest she would turn out to be.

REGENT. British diplomacy at its most hypocritical. Herr Gott, how maddening! To think, that Lucy Maidenhead has been telephoning me every day since my arrival begging me, imploring me to spare her just a few brief moments of my time.

PETER. If I might remind Your Royal Highness, I think I heard you remark the other day that you found Lady Maidenhead—"old hat".

REGENT. I have no doubt at all that I did. Nevertheless, my dear Northbrook, there is an old Russian saying, "Better an old hat than a bare head."

(*A look passes between* PETER *and the* REGENT)

Telephone to Lady Maidenhead and ask her to join me tonight here for supper.

PETER. But, sir—the Foreign Office Ball . . .

REGENT. I shall make an *acte de présence* and leave in good time. Say about twelve thirty.

PETER (*moving to the desk*) Very well, sir. Do you know her telephone number?

REGENT. Ah! Mayfair eight-two-two—no—three-eight-two—no. (*He stops*) Ah, how the years run by! There was a time when those little numerals would have leaped to my lips. (*He sighs*) Hoffman keeps my private list of numbers in his safe.

(PETER *crosses to the double doors and turns*)

PETER. Tonight, sir, Coronation Night—she may well have an engagement.

REGENT (*quietly confident*) She will break it.

(PETER *bows and backs out by the double doors, closing them after him. The* REGENT *finishes his coffee, rises, puts his cup on the table* C, *then stretches himself luxuriously. Apparently oblivious to his danger, he takes a cigarette from the box on the table* C.

MARY *enters down* L. *She is now dressed again in the evening dress we saw her in the night before, and looks fresh and happy. She sees the* REGENT *who is in the process of lighting the cigarette with his back to her, creeps up to him and puts her hand over his eyes*)

MARY (*gaily*) Guess who?

REGENT (*muttering simultaneously*) Herr Gott! (*He backs below the sofa and summons up a smile*)

(MARY *moves to* L *of the Regent*)
Good morning, my dear. And how are you?
  MARY. Well, I felt just a little frail at first—but now, after a bath in that Albert Hall of a bathroom, I feel wonderful. Real wonderful. Oh, darling—(*she throws her arms around his neck*) I'm so happy.

  (*The* REGENT, *smiling a set smile, releases himself*)
What's the matter?
  REGENT. Someone might come in.
  MARY. Sure. This room is Grand Central Station. I found that out last night. Who cares?
  REGENT (*crossly*) But this is the morning. It's different.
  MARY. What's so different about it? Unless maybe it's you.
  REGENT. I assure you, my dear, I am exactly the same person.
  MARY. You're not acting exactly the same way.
  REGENT. But this is the morning.
  MARY (*staring at him*) You keep saying that. I remember from last night the way you tend to repeat yourself.

  (*The* REGENT *turns, embarrassed, from her steady stare*)

(*Quietly*) Now, tell me, darling, is it only late at night that you're such a very lonely person——

  (*The* REGENT *turns and looks at Mary, wincing at each word*)

—that you feel the need to share your life with a pure young woman whose ennobling love and bright faith and glowing self-sacrifice might bring you back to life? Comes the morning and all the universe of pain and joy that lies in that little world "love" just . . .
  REGENT (*interrupting*) Please! Please! I beg you. There are certain phrases which should never be quoted out of context.
  MARY. But the context's the same, isn't it?

  (*The* REGENT *opens his mouth to reply*)

Yes, I know. It's the morning. Can I have some coffee?
  REGENT. There's no cup.
  MARY (*moving to the table* C) I'll have yours. (*She pours herself some coffee. Sunnily*) Well, my darling Grand Duke—it may be morning for you, but it's still dream time for me. On this Coronation Day, nineteen eleven, I've woken up to find myself madly and romantically and joyously in love with you. So there you are.

  (*There is a pause. The* REGENT *crosses and stands below the chair* LC)

  REGENT (*at a loss*) My dear—I am overwhelmed, but I feel it my duty to . . .

MARY (*interrupting*) No, don't go into another long speech. (*She moves to* R *of the Regent and kneels on the chair* LC) It'll probably be utter nonsense, like most of your long speeches last night.

(*The* REGENT *looks surprised*)

No need to raise those pretty eyebrows, my darling. Because, you see, some of the things you said—even though they sounded like Marie Corelli going further than her furthest—were pretty darn true. You do need love in your life. In fact, I've never met anyone who needs it more. (*Brightly*) Well, dear, now you've got it, and good luck to you. (*She raises her coffee cup in a toast*)

REGENT (*automatically*) Cheerioh! (*He crosses to* R *of the sofa*)

MARY. And I'm not going to apologize too much because I gave you very fair warning last night.

REGENT (*moving up* R *of the sofa*) Excuse me—but that warning covered only a certain contingency.

MARY (*surprised*) Well?

REGENT. Let me hasten to assure you that no such contingency took place.

MARY (*thoughtfully*) No?

REGENT. No.

MARY. Well, what *did* happen then? I can remember everything up to the time I said: "O.K. I'll take the fatal step."

REGENT (*shortly*) You took it. It proved fatal, certainly, but not in the usually accepted sense.

MARY. My legs betrayed me?

REGENT. They were all that did.

MARY. Pass-out, huh? (*She gets off the chair and puts her cup on the table* C) Do you know I haven't done that since an applejack party when I was fifteen?

REGENT. Have you not?

MARY. Well, imagine me passing out on you!

REGENT. Imagine.

MARY (*crossing to him*) Oh, you poor man. You poor, poor Regent, you. Oh, darling, I'm so very, very sorry.

REGENT. That is O.K.

MARY. Never mind, my darling. We have years and years and years ahead of us, haven't we? (*She laughs gaily*)

REGENT. Alas, my dear, that is what is so terrible. Most unhappily I must return to Carpathia tomorrow.

MARY. Tomorrow? That's tough, I admit. Well, the minute my show comes off, I'll be right over. That's a promise.

REGENT (*moving down* C) Splendid.

MARY (*crossing to the window*) Oh dear. (*She looks out*) Oh well, it's a lovely day, and it's wonderful to think that we are going to spend some of it together. Aren't we?

REGENT (*moving a little up* C; *carefully*) Well, now, you see—dear Miss Dagenham . . .

MARY. Miss Dagenham? It was "beloved" last night.
REGENT. Well, you see, beloved—in ten minutes' time I have to leave for the Abbey. The ceremony and the procession will last four or five hours. (*He moves up* L *and turns*) I am meeting the Prime Minister at four, and the French Ambassador at five-thirty. At six-thirty I have a reception here, at seven-thirty I go to Dorchester House for a moment, and from there to the Russian Embassy. (*He crosses up* R) At nine I am dining with the Bulgarian Crown Prince and at ten I go to the ball at the Foreign Office, where, of course, I must remain for the rest of the evening. (*Triumphantly*) So, you see, it appears, alas, that there can be no chance whatever . . .
MARY (*crossing above the desk to* R *of him*) I'll tell you what, I'll walk with you from Dorchester House to the Russian Embassy. How's that?
REGENT. Alas, my dear, there is a certain protocol that has to be . . .
MARY. What's protocol?
REGENT. Well—a certain question of formality—carriages—precedence . . . It is impossible for me to walk with you—(*he moves up* L) through crowded streets from Dorchester House to the Russian Embassy.
MARY (*moving up* C) We could walk through the park.
REGENT (*moving to* L *of the table* C) No, alas, my dear, such things are not possible.
MARY (*moving to* R *of the table* C) Don't go on saying "alas" in that phoney way, or I might begin to think you're really glad to get away from me—and then—I warn you—I shall be a fiend. A remorseless fiend.

(PETER *enters by the double doors*)

(*She picks up her coffee*) Here we go. Grand Central. (*To Peter*) Good morning.
PETER. Good morning, Miss Dagenham. (*He moves above the chair* LC. *Tactfully*) What a pleasant surprise.
MARY (*sitting on the sofa at the left end*) I don't know what's a surprise about it. How's poor old auntie this morning?

(PETER *laughs mirthlessly and exchanges a glance with the* REGENT *who silently indicates that he is going to leave Peter to cope with the situation*)

REGENT (*crossing up* RC) My dear—I must go and get ready. (*He looks at Peter*) So—alas—I mean, I'm afraid—we must say our little adieus. (*He moves to the desk and opens a drawer*)
MARY. Oh, no. Not till the last possible second. Not till you actually leave this building.

(*The* REGENT *closes the drawer*)

And it won't be *adieu*. It'll be *au revoir*.

REGENT (*with a sigh*) Yes. Well . . . (*He goes quickly to the door down* R)

(MARY *continues placidly drinking her coffee. There is a shocked hiss from* PETER *at this breach of etiquette*)

PETER. Miss Dagenham.

MARY. Oh, gosh! Do we have to go through all that again? (*She rises and drops the Regent a very graceful curtsy*) Your Royal Highness.

(*In the street a barrel-organ can be heard playing music from "The Coconut Girl"*).

REGENT (*helplessly*) Pray be seated, Miss Dagenham.

(*The* REGENT *exits down* R. MARY *resumes her seat on the sofa*)

MARY (*feeling her knees*) A little hard on the knee muscles these royal circles. Say listen—could you find me an old raincoat or something?

PETER (*moving to* L *of Mary*) An old raincoat?

MARY. Sure. I've paid two pounds for a seat on the balcony outside of the *Haymarket Theatre*, and I can't turn up in an evening dress, with Maisie and the whole gang there.

PETER. Very well. I shall see if I can find you an old raincoat, but such things are not so easy to come by as you may think in Belgrave Square. Let me see now. Perhaps one of the kitchen staff . . .

(PETER *exits by the double doors.*
The jaunty little tune from the barrel-organ is plainly recognizable to Mary. She begins to sing absent-mindedly to herself)

MARY.   They call me The Coconut Girl:
                No mediocre nut girl

(*She gets up to put her cup down on the table* C, *and slips in to a dance routine of the period, singing the while*)
                Two shies a penny,
                And I've been offered many
                A ruby or a pearl.
                You may be coconut shy
                Do say you'll give me a try.
                Walk up, walk up, commoner or earl
                Ev'ry bloke likes a joke with the coconut girl.

(NICOLAS *enters by the double doors.* MARY, *dancing down* L *and then across to* R, *does not see him until she turns. She stops on recognizing him*)

MARY. Oh, it's you. I mean it's Your Majesty. (*She curtsies*)

Scene 2   THE SLEEPING PRINCE   39

NICOLAS. Good morning, Miss Dagenham. What is that dance?
MARY (*flustered*) Well, it's a new routine. You wouldn't understand what that means—but it's something I have to practise. Your Majesty is probably wondering why I'm still wearing the same dress as last night. The fact is I had a stupid accident with my latch-key and so a bed had to be found for me in the Legation.
NICOLAS (*with perfect, if slightly bored, politeness*) Of course. (*He closes the door*) What could be more natural? Where is my father?
MARY (*indicating the door down* R) In there, getting ready.
NICOLAS (*eagerly*) Has he just gone in?
MARY. A moment ago.
NICOLAS (*crossing to* L *of Mary*) Miss Dagenham, may I ask you to do a small favour for me?
MARY. I should be delighted.
NICOLAS. Will you ring up a certain telephone number—(*he takes a slip of paper from his pocket*) this one. (*He hands the paper to Mary*)
MARY (*moving to the desk and lifting the telephone receiver*) What could be easier?

   (NICOLAS *moves slowly up* RC)

(*Into the telephone*) Hullo . . . Gerrard two-four-five, please . . .
NICOLAS (*eagerly*) Ask for the Ambassador.

   (MARY *nods*)

MARY (*into the telephone*) Hullo . . . Give me the Ambassador please . . . Well, it's not me, it's the King of Carpathia . . .
NICOLAS (*grabbing the receiver and putting his hand over the mouthpiece*) You shouldn't have said that. There are spies everywhere.
MARY. Oh. Are there? It's him. (*She hands the telephone to Nicolas, then leans against the downstage corner of the window*)
NICOLAS (*into the telephone; in a quick low voice*) Euer Exzellenz. Ich werde standigt beobachtet. Sie sind der einzige durch den ich eine Nachricht senden kann. Dies ist an General Ravinof weiterzul eiten. "In Anbetracht der letzten Entwicklungen fallt die entscheidung auf Datum eins", Datum eins. Jawohl. Auf Widersehen. (*He replaces the receiver, carefully putting it down so that no ring shall be audible, then crosses above the sofa towards the double doors. To Mary*) I shall not soon forget your kindness in this matter, Miss Dagenham.
MARY. Think nothing of it.

   (NICOLAS *exits by the double doors*)

(*She moves to the desk and lifts the receiver. Into the telephone*) I want another number, please. Brixton nine-three-seven . . . (*She sits on the right edge of the desk and puts her feet on the desk chair*) Hullo, Fanny . . . Hiya . . . Were you worried about me? . . . Well, it's a long story . . . No, darling, that'd be a *short* story. This is a *long* one . . . Listen, don't tell the gang a thing, will you? . . .

    (*The* REGENT *enters down* R. *He is dressed for the Coronation in a very grandiose uniform, with many trimmings*)

(*She does not see the Regent. Into the telephone*) Sure I'm coming. I wouldn't miss it for the world. Besides, *he*'ll be in the procession . . . Oh, he's the cutest little Grand Duke in the world . . . No. Not really handsome, just sort of cute . . . Oh, no. (*She gets down off the desk and stands with her back to the room*)

    (*The* REGENT *crosses and stands above the sofa*)

Not at all like the Grand Dukes you see on the stage . . . No sense of humour, no charm, not much manners, but for all that I love him so much I could eat him. Chew him up . . . Yes, darling. I'll tell you all about it later. Don't forget now—not a word. Bye. (*She replaces the receiver, turns and sees the Regent*)

    REGENT (*very angrily*) But I have a very good sense of humour.

    MARY (*soothingly*) Yes, darling. Of course you have—only it's a kind of Balkan one. (*She leans on the back of the desk chair*) Just as good as Anglo-Saxon, I'm sure, but different. Anyway, you shouldn't listen to private telephone conversations.

    (*The* REGENT *crosses to the desk, opens a drawer, gets out a small jewel box and brusquely hands it to Mary*)

What's this?

    REGENT (*moving down* RC) A small parting gift. I was going to present it to you with a few appropriate words, but now you have driven them clean out of my head.

    MARY (*opening the box and taking out a brooch*) Say, this is beautiful—(*she moves below the desk*) with your crest and everything.

    REGENT (*moving down* C; *brusquely*) It is nothing.

    MARY. I'm not looking a gift horse, but I'll bet there are quite a few of these being worn round Europe, huh? (*She crosses to* R *of the sofa*) Say—not Maisie Springfield . . .

    REGENT. No. She got a snuff-box.

    MARY. Gee. I guess this rates higher than hers, then.

    REGENT (*moving below the chair* LC) It was a Fabergé snuff-box—in rubies and emeralds.

    MARY. Oh. (*With a shrug*) Oh well, I can't complain. After all, she really earned hers. Here. (*She crosses to* R *of him*) Pin it on. (*She indicates to him where she wants him to pin the brooch*)

    (*The* REGENT *pins the brooch on Mary's dress*)

(*She looks down, suddenly rather sad, at the top of his head*) So this is where I wake up, is it?

    REGENT. I fear so, my dear.

Scene 2   THE SLEEPING PRINCE   41

MARY (*staring at him*) Pity. Well—all I can say is that for a good-bye scene you've got quite the wrong costume on.
REGENT. What is the matter with it?
MARY. Nothing. Nothing at all. That's the trouble.
REGENT. It makes me look—cute?
MARY. I'll say.
REGENT. Almost like a Grand Duke on the stage?
MARY. Almost.

(*The* REGENT *smiles and glances briefly at his watch*)

Yes. O.K. That's my cue. Good-bye.
REGENT (*moving to her*) It has been wonderful knowing you. (*He gives her a tender kiss*) If only it could have lasted longer.

(MARY *starts suddenly to giggle, and steps back*)

What is the matter? Have I said anything wrong?
MARY. No. You spoke the line beautifully. It was your medals. They were tickling me.
REGENT (*angrily*) Why are you always saying such things? (*He crosses to the double doors and knocks on them*) You seem to enjoy disconcerting me—and that is one thing I cannot bear—to be disconcerted.

(PETER *enters by the double doors. He carries a raincoat*)

(*To Peter*) I am spending two minutes with the Minister. Join us in the hall. (*He turns and bows to Mary*) Good-bye, again.
MARY (*with a curtsy*) Your Royal Highness.

(*The* REGENT *exits by the double doors. The* FOOTMEN, *outside, close the doors.* PETER *crosses above the sofa to* R *of Mary*)

PETER. This is all I could find, I'm afraid. It belongs to a scullery maid.
MARY. It'll do very well.

(PETER *helps* MARY *into the raincoat, which is old and rather shabby*).

(*She collects her bag from the sofa. With a sigh*) Oh dear! Life's rather sad sometimes, isn't it?
PETER. Sometimes.
MARY. I'll never get a taxi or anything now. I'll have to walk. Oh well . . . (*She crosses to the double doors*)

(PETER *follows Mary to* C. *The double doors are opened by the* FOOTMEN.
    The GRAND DUCHESS *enters by the double doors. She is in full regalia.*
    MARY *turns tail and flees through the door down* L, *closing it behind her*)

GRAND DUCHESS (*moving down* LC) Who was that? Mr Northbrook, who was that creature? Was it an anarchist?
PETER. No, ma'am.
GRAND DUCHESS. Well, who was it?
PETER. A young lady, ma'am, called Miss Elaine Dagenham.
GRAND DUCHESS (*sitting in the chair* LC) Fetch her to me.

(PETER *crosses to the door down* L, *opens it and beckons.*
MARY *comes timidly in and curtsies to the* GRAND DUCHESS, *who holds out her hand.* PETER *stands behind the chair* LC)

Good morning, my dear? So delightful to see you again. Why are you dressed up as a revolutionary? Is this a new game? If it is you should have let me know. I love games.
MARY. It isn't a game, ma'am.
GRAND DUCHESS. Well, take that thing off. It looks most unbecoming.

(MARY *takes off the raincoat and rolls it up, revealing her evening dress, of which the* GRAND DUCHESS *seems utterly oblivious*)

And please sit down.

(MARY *sits on the edge of the chair down* L)

I am going to have a cigarette.

(PETER *moves to the table* C *and picks up the cigarette box and matches*)

So soothing before a long ordeal. Will you join me?
MARY. No, thank you, ma'am.

(PETER *offers the Grand Duchess a cigarette, and lights it for her.*
MARY *stuffs the raincoat behind her chair*)

(*Acutely conscious of her attire*) Your Imperial and Royal Highness is probably wondering why I'm still dressed as I was last night. The fact is I had a stupid accident with my latch-key...
GRAND DUCHESS (*to Peter*) What does she say?
PETER. She says she had an accident with her latch-key...
GRAND DUCHESS. Latch-key? What is a latch-key?
PETER. Well, ma'am, it's...
GRAND DUCHESS. It doesn't matter. I'm sure it's something very dull. (*Still to Peter*) Such irritating news, Mr Northbrook, this morning. Maud von und zu Meissenbronn—my chief lady-in-waiting—claims she cannot leave her bed, so I have no option but to take the Baroness Brunheim to the Abbey, which means we shall all be very squashed in the carriage. So maddening of Maud —this morning of all mornings.
PETER. I trust that there is nothing seriously wrong with her?
GRAND DUCHESS. Nothing at all. Last night she had a slight

head cold, so I dosed her with one of my syrups. This morning she announces the cold has left her head and descended to her stomach. Imagine. (*To Mary*) Je ne sais pas pourquoi, mais les madadies des autres m'embêtent toujours, surtout si elles sont imaginaires, comme celles de la Comtesse—vous trouvez ça aussi?

(*There is a pause*)

MARY (*at length*) Excuse me, ma'am, I didn't quite catch what you said.

GRAND DUCHESS (*to Peter*) Yes?

PETER. I don't think Miss Dagenham speaks French, ma'am.

GRAND DUCHESS. Doesn't speak French? Ridiculous! She lives with Madame Bernhardt in Paris. (*To Mary*) N'est-ce pas, ma petite? Je suis sûre que vous parlez le français mieux qu'une Française, et surtout d'une voix d'or.

MARY (*at length*) Oui.

GRAND DUCHESS (*to Peter*) You see. (*To Mary*) Au sujet des maladies des autres, c'était La Rochefoucauld, n'est-ce pas, qui a dit: "dans l'adversité de nos meilleurs amis, nous trouvons quelque chose qui ne nous déplait pas?"

MARY (*at length*) Oui.

GRAND DUCHESS. Eh, bien, je vous assure que dans les advertsités de Maud, je ne trouve jamais rien qui ne me déplait pas infiniment. (*She laughs*)

(MARY, *taking the cue, laughs too*)

(*She turns and gives her half-finished cigarette to Peter*) Most intelligent. Reading Rochefoucauld.

(PETER *stubs out the cigarette in the ashtray on the table* C)

Mr Northbrook, please tell Baroness Brunheim to bring me my jewel box.

(PETER *bows and exits by the double doors, leaving them open.* MARY *stares at the Grand Duchess, like a rabbit at a snake. She breathes a sigh of relief as the* GRAND DUCHESS *resumes her conversation in English*)

My dear, I hear there are great multitudes in the streets, and all being so enthusiastic and loyal that even the soldiers have turned their backs to the people, and are facing the procession. Most gratifying. Isn't that an evening dress you are wearing?

MARY (*helplessly*) Yes, ma'am. I was trying to explain...

GRAND DUCHESS. Stand up and let me see it. Walk across here, please.

(MARY *rises and walks across to* RC)

(*She watches Mary*) Excellent. Most suitable. Now what was I saying?

MARY. About the crowds being so loyal, ma'am.
GRAND DUCHESS. Oh, yes. Such a change from the last Coronation I attended—the Bessarabias. My dear—only the merest trickle of people in the streets, revolver shots going off like kettledrums and the sky black with infernal machines.

(*The* BARONESS BRUNHEIM *and* PETER *enter by the double doors. The* BARONESS *is a plumpish lady of middle age, dressed for the Abbey. She carries a large jewel case*)

Happily no fatalities—except in the crowd—but it all left a very bad impression. And the service—far too long and the singing really not at all good. Not good at all. (*She rises*) Ah, Lottie, put it there. (*She indicates the chair* LC) Thank you, Mr Northbrook.

(PETER *bows and exits by the double doors. The* BARONESS *puts the jewel box on the chair* LC *and opens it*)

(*She takes a pearl choker from the jewel box and approaches Mary*) Just stand still, dear. (*She fastens the choker on Mary's neck, then stands back to survey the result*) Yes. That is very possible. (*She takes a diamond necklace from the jewel box*) We need this, too, of course. (*She puts the necklace around Mary's neck*)
MARY. What is happening, ma'am. Is this a game, ma'am?
GRAND DUCHESS. What did you say, my dear?
MARY (*to the Baroness*) Ask ma'am is this a game.
BARONESS (*to the Grand Duchess*) She wants to know, ma'am, is this a game?
GRAND DUCHESS (*to the Baroness*) Lottie, my dear, put your cape on her, would you?

(*The* BARONESS *removes her fur cape, crosses to* R *of Mary and puts the cape on her*)

MARY. Please, what is happening?
GRAND DUCHESS. Better and better. (*She turns to the Baroness*) Lottie, will you be very disappointed . . . ?
BARONESS (*with a beaming smile*) Oh, but that is perfectly all right, ma'am. As you know—with my trouble—I always *have* been a little nervous of long ceremonies.
GRAND DUCHESS. Good. That is settled, then. (*To the Baroness*) Arrange your veil on her, and lend her your gloves.

(*The* BARONESS *puts her veil on Mary's head, gives Mary her gloves, then collects the jewel box, crosses and puts it on the desk chair*)

MARY (*bewildered*) Please tell me, ma'am? What's going on?
GRAND DUCHESS (*moving below the chair* LC) I am appointing you my lady-in-waiting for the day, my dear, and taking you to the Abbey.
MARY. But, ma'am, you can't. I mean, someone will recognize me, and I shall be arrested.

GRAND DUCHESS (*in icy tones*) Arrest my lady-in-waiting? My dear child! (*She turns and moves below the table* L) Such an imbecility!
MARY (*in a frenzy*) But what do I do? Where do I sit?
GRAND DUCHESS (*impatiently*) Just do what I do, and sit next to me. (*She turns and looks at Mary*) You still look a little bare. I know. You need an Order.

(*The* REGENT *enters by the double doors and stands just inside the doorway*)

REGENT. Is it time—that we . . . (*He is suddenly transfixed by the sight of the now nearly transformed Mary*)
MARY. Hullo.
GRAND DUCHESS (*moving to the Regent*) My dear, such fun! How you will roar. We are taking Miss Dagenham to the Abbey.

(*There is a pause*)

REGENT (*at length*) Oh? Are we?
GRAND DUCHESS (*crossing to the table* C) I need an Order for her, my dear. (*To the Baroness*) What is that one you are wearing, Lottie? The Purple Pillow? No, that would hardly suit. I know —that nice mauve one—what is it called—(*to the Regent*) you know the one I mean, my dear, the one you gave to the Foreign Secretary the other day. So fetching. Give her that. (*To the Baroness*) Lottie—in that bureau there—the centre drawer. Hand it to the Regent.

(*The* BARONESS *moves to the desk and takes a case from the centre drawer*)

(*She looks at Mary*) We will now be most comfortable in the carriage.

(*The* BARONESS *offers the case to the* REGENT, *who opens it and takes out the Order. The* BARONESS *then returns the case to the desk and stands* R *of the sofa*)

REGENT (*moving to* L *of the Grand Duchess*) You realize, no doubt, that this Order is only given for a very special personal service to the head of the State. (*He moves below the sofa*)
GRAND DUCHESS (*impatiently*) Such hair-splitting! No doubt she will do you one, one day.
REGENT (*to Mary*) Take your cape off.

(*The* BARONESS *removes Mary's cape and holds it for her*)

Kneel down.

(MARY *kneels* R *of the Regent*)

I hereby invest you with the Royal Carpathian Order of Perseverance, second class. (*He pins the ribbon on Mary, kisses her brow, then crosses below her to* R)

(MARY *rises. The* BARONESS *puts the cape on Mary's shoulders, then moves up* R. MARY *takes off her brooch*)

GRAND DUCHESS (*moving to the double doors*) Come, my dears.

MARY (*turning to the Regent*) And I hereby return you this. (*She hands him the brooch*) After all, we're not parting quite yet—are we, my darling? (*She curtsies to him*)

The REGENT, *his face expressionless, crosses to the double doors and joins the Grand Duchess.* MARY *shrugs her shoulders, happily, and follows them off as—*

the CURTAIN *falls*

ACT II

Scene I

Scene—*The same. About 7 p.m. of the same day.*

When the Curtain *rises, the* Grand Duchess *is reclining on the sofa, with her feet up, her head to* L. *On the floor beside her is a large box of chocolates, into which she is occasionally dipping.* Mary *is seated on a footstool below the right end of the sofa, engaged in reading aloud. Both ladies are wearing the clothes in which they had been to the Abbey that morning.*

Mary (*reading*) "At this juncture the prisoner asked for a glass of water which was given to him by a warder. Mr Muir—resuming his cross-examination—'Now, Dr Crippen, kindly tell the jury why it was that you pawned your wife's jewels?' Dr Crippen, 'Because I needed some new dental instruments.' 'Was that an urgent matter?' 'No.' 'Then why were you in such a hurry to pawn your wife's ear-rings and marquise rings?'"

Grand Duchess. There are photographs of these jewels, are there not?

Mary. Yes, ma'am. (*She hands the book to the Grand Duchess*)

Grand Duchess (*carefully inspecting the photographs*) Most disappointing. Plainly not the motive. (*She returns the book to Mary*) Go on, dear, I want to get on to the summing-up. So many holes in the evidence—such fun.

Mary (*reading*) "Dr Crippen—'I don't know.' Mr Muir— 'Was the money so raised to enable you to flee the country?' 'Yes.' 'Under a false name?' 'Yes.' 'Having shaved off your moustache?' 'Yes.' 'Taking Miss le Neve away with you?' 'Yes.' 'Disguised as a boy?' 'Yes.' 'Posing as your son?' 'I cannot deny it.'"

(*The* Regent *enters down* R. *He is wearing a different uniform. He glances at Mary and moves above the head of the sofa.* Mary *stops reading and stares at him with open admiration, then remembering herself, hastily rises, still staring, and moves up* R *of the sofa*)

Grand Duchess. My dear—so much noise and confusion downstairs. The Minister is giving a reception for some wretchedly dull people, and when, to cap the horror, they announced the arrival of that dreadful Archduchess Ferdinand and her idiotic daughter, I simply flew up here.

Regent. But, my dear, I wanted you to be particularly polite to Maria and Louisa this afternoon. It is most important.

Grand Duchess. Important? For what reason?

REGENT (*patiently*) I have told you many times of our plans for Louisa and Nicky.

GRAND DUCHESS. So you have. So you have. I keep forgetting. (*After a moment's cogitation*) Yes. Most suitable, I suppose. Most suitable. A pity she is such a horrid little brat and has such dreadful parents, but I agree that in every other way the match is ideal. Very well, my dear. (*She swings her feet off the sofa*) I shall not shirk my duty.

REGENT (*crossing to the double doors and turning*) Why don't you receive them here? And I shall send Nicky up to join you. Where is he?

GRAND DUCHESS. Now where is Nicky? I saw him somewhere, I know. Oh, yes. He was in the garden, kicking something.

REGENT (*moving above the chair* LC; *alarmed*) Kicking? Kicking what?

GRAND DUCHESS (*to* MARY) What was it the King was kicking, dear?

MARY. A football.

GRAND DUCHESS. Yes, that's what it was. A football. Dear Miss Dagenham. She has been such a help to me all day, Charles. I can hardly tell you how good she has been.

(*A look passes between* MARY *and the* REGENT)

REGENT. I'm so glad. (*Finding Mary's eyes on him he self-consciously tugs at his uniform jacket to hide a crease*)

(MARY *nods approvingly, her eyes never wavering from him*)

GRAND DUCHESS. Reads most prettily, too. Of course with such a dramatic training one would expect that. And so intelligent and erudite, Charles. Do you know that there is hardly a French author whom she has not read. To every name I give her she just answers "Oui".

(*A look passes between* MARY *and the* REGENT)

So modest and charming. And looked most handsome at the Abbey, I thought—didn't you, my dear?

REGENT. Most handsome.

GRAND DUCHESS. I am happy to tell you that I have succeeded in wringing a promise from her to pay us a long visit to Carpathia. Isn't that good?

(MARY *moves a step or two up* RC)

REGENT. Quite splendid. (*He moves to the double doors and knocks on them*) Well, I must collect Maria and . . .

(*The* FOOTMEN *open the double doors*)

My dear, we mustn't be selfish and keep Miss Dagenham too long.

(*He looks at his watch*) I fear she will have to leave us very soon for her theatre. So sad.

(*The* REGENT *exits by the double doors, which are closed by the* FOOTMEN)

GRAND DUCHESS. Theatre? What theatre? Are you giving something tonight, my dear? I had no idea.

MARY (*moving to* R *of the sofa*) Yes, Ma'am.

GRAND DUCHESS. But how exciting! What are you giving?

MARY (*turning away; in a small voice*) *The Coconut Girl.*

GRAND DUCHESS. I didn't quite catch that, my dear. Speak a little more clearly. What is the name of your role?

MARY (*turning*) Fifi.

GRAND DUCHESS. Fifi? Ah yes. Of course, I know it well. By Sardou, I think?

MARY (*accustomed to this by now*) Er, no, ma'am.

GRAND DUCHESS. Who is it by, then?

MARY (*with resignation*) Al Fleischberg, Buddy Maxwell and Joe Zink.

GRAND DUCHESS (*after a moment's reflection*) I do not think I know these authors.

MARY. They are American, ma'am.

GRAND DUCHESS. American? *Tiens!* They have theatre in America, too?

MARY. Oh yes, ma'am.

GRAND DUCHESS. How strange! And this "Fifi", of these authors, you are giving it tonight as a special performance?

MARY. No, ma'am. It's already been running for over a year.

GRAND DUCHESS. A year! My dear. Such a role, so many times. How dreadfully tired you must be. Please sit down.

(MARY *sits* R *of the Grand Duchess on the sofa*)

I remember once at Furstenstein we gave *King Lear* to the villagers and foresters, and we were so successful that dear Daisy insisted we should give it again the next night for the gamekeepers and huntsmen. But, my dear. So exhausted were we all that we had to cancel the performance, although the money had been paid and the seats engaged. Only the man who acted Lear wanted to do it again, but as he was a professional actor there was, of course, no effort for him to remember his words, like the rest of us. You know *King Lear*?

MARY. Not well, ma'am.

GRAND DUCHESS. A most delightful little play. Quite touching and very little love. I acted the part of Kent—we had not enough men as usual—but everyone was most kind, and said I made a very handsome boy. I was quite word perfect and made only one mistake—when I was talking to Princess Schlumberger-Lippe-Gildenstern about her poor husband—such a worry to us all—

and, my dear, I quite forgot to go on to the stage for the scene where I am put in the stocks. However, the Duke of Stirling who was acting the steward most ingeniously saved the situation by saying some of my words as well as his, omitting the fight and sitting in the stocks himself. So quick-witted and nothing was noticed—but, of course, the majority of our audience only spoke German, and we were acting, naturally, in English ...

(*The double doors are opened by the* FOOTMEN.
The MAJOR-DOMO *enters and stands above the doors*)

(*She rises. Hastily*) What time must you leave for your theatre?
MARY (*rising*) In about twenty minutes, ma'am.
GRAND DUCHESS (*moving* L *of the chair* LC) Stay with me through this.

(MARY *picks up the box of chocolates, moves to the desk, puts the box on it, then stands above the right end of the sofa*)

MAJOR-DOMO (*announcing*) Her Royal Highness the Archduchess Ferdinand of Styria. Her Royal Highness the Princess Louisa.

(HER ROYAL HIGHNESS, THE ARCHDUCHESS FERDINAND OF STYRIA, *and* HER ROYAL HIGHNESS, THE PRINCESS LOUISA OF STYRIA *enter by the double doors*, LOUISA L *of the* ARCHDUCHESS, *who is large and red-faced*. LOUISA, *her daughter, a girl of about fifteen, is an angry-looking child in pigtails. The two* DUCHESSES, *grand and arch, meet with a loving kiss, on both cheeks*. LOUISA *curtsies*.

The MAJOR-DOMO *exits, the* FOOTMEN *closing the double doors after him*)

GRAND DUCHESS. Dear Maria! So delightful. And how handsome little Louisa has become.
ARCHDUCHESS (*a shade truculently*) Did you not think her handsome before?
GRAND DUCHESS. My dear, there are degrees in these things. (*She ushers them* C) Shall we sit down? This is Miss Dagenham, the actress. You have heard of her, of course.
ARCHDUCHESS. Of course.

(LOUISA *crosses to* RC)

Many times. (*She sits on the sofa*)
LOUISA (*with a step towards Mary; suspiciously*) What are you acting in?
GRAND DUCHESS (*sitting in the chair* LC) At the moment she is giving the Fifi of Fleischberg, Maxwell and Zink.
LOUISA (*crossing to the chair down* R *and sitting*) I've never heard of it.
GRAND DUCHESS (*sharply*) Then you should have done. (*To* MARY) Give the Princess a chocolate, dear.

(MARY *moves to the desk, picks up the box of chocolates and proffers it to* LOUISA, *who takes one.* MARY *is about to move away, but* LOUISA *summons her imperiously back, and takes two more*)

And how is your dear husband?

ARCHDUCHESS. Oh, Ferdinand is very well.

GRAND DUCHESS (*to* MARY; *noticing* LOUISA'S *grabbing of the chocolates*) Bring the chocolates here, dear.

(MARY *crosses to* L *of the sofa*)

(*To the Archduchess*) Would you care . . . ?

(MARY *turns and proffers the box to the* ARCHDUCHESS, *who shakes her head.* MARY *puts the box on the table* C, *then crosses above the chair* LC *to* L *of it*)

(*She firmly places the lid on the box*) The same irrepressible high spirits?

ARCHDUCHESS. My dear—the other day, at a restaurant in Paris—how you would have roared. He sat down at the table with his hat on his head, and when the maître-d'hôtel came up and said, "May I take Your Royal Highness' hat," he said, "Yes, and you can take your soup, too." And with that he poured his soup into his hat and handed it to the maître-d'hôtel. My dear—the man's face—it was a study. (*She laughs uproariously*)

(*The* GRAND DUCHESS *is stony-faced*)

GRAND DUCHESS. You know my little affliction.

(*The* ARCHDUCHESS *stops laughing*)

Excuse me. (*To* MARY) Yes, dear?

MARY. The Archduchess's husband . . .

GRAND DUCHESS. The Archduke Ferdinand, dear. Such a witty man. Go on.

MARY (*in a low voice; she has learnt the trick*) The Archduke Ferdinand sat down at a table in a restaurant in Paris with his hat on his head. When the head waiter asked him for his hat he said you can have the hat and the soup, too. So then he poured the soup into the hat and handed it to the head waiter—whose face, the Archduchess said, was a study.

(*There is a short pause*)

GRAND DUCHESS (*at length; to the Archduchess*) Incomparable.

ARCHDUCHESS. You remember when he went to the Serbian Legation in a false beard?

GRAND DUCHESS (*to* MARY) Yes?

MARY (*in her interpreting voice*) The Archduchess asks if you remember when the Archduke went to the Serbian Legation in a false beard.

GRAND DUCHESS (*to the Archduchess*) Vividly.
ARCHDUCHESS. And half of it fell off in the soup? (*She laughs*)

(*The* GRAND DUCHESS *glances enquiringly at* MARY)

MARY. And half of the false beard fell off in the soup.
GRAND DUCHESS (*at length*) Irresistible. And whose hat did he put that in? I forget now.
ARCHDUCHESS. No, no. He didn't put it in anyone's hat. He called the head butler over and said, "I think you have given me hare soup." Hare soup, do you see? H-A-I-R and H-A-R-E.

(MARY *bends forward to repeat but the* GRAND DUCHESS *waves her back*)

GRAND DUCHESS. Thank you, dear. I heard that.

(*The double doors are opened by the* FOOTMEN.
The MAJOR-DOMO *enters by the double doors and stands above them*)

MAJOR-DOMO (*announcing*) His Majesty.

(*All rise, the* ARCHDUCHESS *and* LOUISA *both rather unwillingly it seems.*
NICOLAS *enters by the double doors and crosses to the Archduchess. He is looking regal in a uniform, with orders.*
The MAJOR-DOMO *exits, the* FOOTMEN *closing the double doors behind him*)

NICOLAS. How are you, Aunt Maria? (*He kisses both her cheeks*)
ARCHDUCHESS (*with a curtsy*) Very well, thank you, Nicky.
NICOLAS (*crossing to Louisa*) And Cousin Louisa?

(LOUISA *turns her face downstage, and* NICOLAS *kisses her left cheek, then* LOUISA *turns her face upstage, but* NICOLAS *only pats her arm*)

Won't you sit down?

(*The* ARCHDUCHESS *and* LOUISA *resume their seats*)

GRAND DUCHESS. My dear, I know how eager you are to talk to dear little Louisa, and I must not be selfish and keep your Aunt Maria any longer from the reception downstairs.

(NICOLAS *crosses to the double doors, knocks on them, then moves down* L)

(*She moves above the chair* LC. *To the Archduchess*) So, my dear, shall I deliver you again into the hands of our Minister, who I know is furious with me already for stealing you?

(*The* ARCHDUCHESS *and* LOUISA *rise*)

ARCHDUCHESS. There will be a chaperone for the young people?

THE SLEEPING PRINCE

GRAND DUCHESS (*moving to the double doors*) Miss Dagenham will stay.

(*The* ARCHDUCHESS *turns and picks up her gloves from the sofa. The* FOOTMEN *open the double doors*)

MARY. But, ma'am, I should be going . . .

(NICOLAS *takes a sudden quick step towards Mary*)

GRAND DUCHESS (*turning to Mary*) Did you say something, dear?

(*The* ARCHDUCHESS *moves to the double doors*)

MARY (*with a curtsy*) Nothing, ma'am.

GRAND DUCHESS (*to the Archduchess*) I wonder if dear Ferdinand does not nurture some strange fascination for soup. I notice so many of his most brilliant escapades are connected with it.

(*The* GRAND DUCHESS *and the* ARCHDUCHESS *exit by the double doors*)

(*As she goes*) Ah, but of course, I was forgetting the famous incident with the lemon meringue at Homburg . . .

(*The* FOOTMEN *close the double doors. There is a pause.* LOUISA *turns downstage, points her foot and just looks sullen.* NICOLAS *is plainly diffident and embarrassed. He coughs.* LOUISA *glances at him for a moment, then turns away*)

NICOLAS (*moving above the table* C; *to Louisa*) Won't you sit down?

LOUISA. No, thank you. (*She crosses to the footstool below the sofa and stands on it*)

(NICOLAS *crosses to the window*)

NICOLAS (*turning*) Shall we talk in English, oder sollen wir Deutsch sprechen? Ou Français, si vous préférez.

LOUISA. That is just boasting. I speak seven languages. (*She steps off the stool*)

(MARY *moves* C)

NICOLAS (*politely*) Very clever. (*After a pause*) I speak eight.

LOUISA (*crossing to the table* L) You are older, and Carpathian hardly counts. (*She puts her hat and gloves on the table, and picks up a magazine*)

NICOLAS (*hotly*) Why not? What is the matter with my native tongue?

LOUISA. A patois.

NICOLAS (*moving to the desk; furious*) Patois be . . .

MARY (*moving up* C; *restrainingly*) Sir.

NICOLAS (*murmuring*) Yes. (*After a pause, with his back half turned towards the others*) Are you going to the ball tonight?

LOUISA. That is just boasting, too. You know I can't go. I don't know why they let you go.

NICOLAS (*turning to face the others*) I go to balls in my own country.

LOUISA (*moving to the chair down* L; *in tones of faint scorn*) Do they have balls in Carpathia? I thought it was all lederhosen, bare knees and slapping each other. (*She sits*)

(NICOLAS *takes a breath to reply in kind.* MARY *gestures.* NICOLAS *nods*)

I've sat down. You did ask me to. Anyway, I think such things are stupid. (*She appears deeply interested in the magazine*)

NICOLAS (*moving and sitting in the chair down* R) I agree. (*Dutifully*) Cousin Louisa . . . (*He stops uncertainly*)

LOUISA (*deep in the magazine*) Cousin Nicolas?

(*There is a pause*)

(*She looks at Nicolas over the edge of her magazine*) There's really no need to say what you are going to say, unless you particularly want to. I'll tell my mother you said it, and you can tell your father I made the right answer. It's not for eighteen months, anyway—is it?

NICOLAS. No.

LOUISA (*intent on her magazine*) So that's all right.

NICOLAS (*after a pause*) I find that rather sensible.

LOUISA. I *am* sensible.

(*There is a long pause, while* LOUISA *buries herself deeper in her magazine.* MARY, *plainly shocked at what she has heard, looks at the clock*)

MARY (*moving above the sofa*) Look—I wonder whether you two really *need* a chaperone?

NICOLAS. Don't go, please, unless you have to. (*He rises*)

MARY. Well, Your Majesty . . .

NICOLAS. I heard you went to the Coronation with my stepmother? What did you think of it?

MARY. The greatest experience of my life—that's all.

NICOLAS. You must come to mine.

MARY (*moving up* R *of the sofa*) I should like to very much, sir, always provided you haven't put your father in some deep dungeon by then.

(NICOLAS *looks quickly over his shoulder to* L)

NICOLAS (*with a step towards Mary*) That is a good joke, Miss Dagenham.

MARY. Is it such a joke? I'm remembering a little telephone conversation from this morning.

NICOLAS (*defensively*) I was talking to the German Ambassador about an invitation to a shooting party.
MARY (*moving to the table* R) Shooting party may be right. I happen to speak German, you know. I was born in Milwaukee.
LOUISA (*lowering her magazine*) What are you two talking about?
NICOLAS (*with a step towards Louisa*) You wouldn't be interested.
LOUISA. I might be. What was it?
NICOLAS. Miss Dagenham was telling me about where she was born.
LOUISA (*into her magazine*) No. I wouldn't be.
NICOLAS (*turning to Mary*) All right. If you speak German give me an English translation of what I said.
MARY (*leaning against the table* R) Let's see. "For relay to General Ravinof. In view of recent developments, date one." Right?
NICOLAS (*moving below the desk*) You've told father, of course?
MARY. No.
NICOLAS (*turning to Mary*) But you're going to?
MARY. No.
NICOLAS. Why not?
MARY. Never mind.

(LOUISA *rises, moves to the table* L, *exchanges her magazine for another, then moves to the door down* L)

Just take it I won't.
LOUISA. What is this room?
NICOLAS (*crossing to* R *of the sofa*) A bedroom.
LOUISA. I think I will read in here. I cannot concentrate when there is talking.

(LOUISA *exits down* L)

NICOLAS. Odious girl.
MARY. Agreed. (*She laughs*)

(NICOLAS *laughs.* MARY *crosses below the sofa as if to leave*)

NICOLAS. It is good of you not to give me away to father. I am grateful.
MARY (*stopping* C *and turning*) I have one proviso, though. A serious one, and on this you must give me your kingly oath, or whatever it is. You don't intend him any harm?
NICOLAS (*turning and facing down* R; *carefully*) If he agrees to the changed situation, he may remain in Carpathia without let or hindrance, and with all due rights and honours.
MARY. And if he disagrees?
NICOLAS (*after a pause; moving to the desk*) He must live outside Carpathia.
MARY. Exile, in fact?
NICOLAS. Well . . .

MARY (*moving to* R *of the chair* LC; *warmly*) But, Nicky, for heaven's sake, the guy's your pa!

(NICOLAS *turns, with regal dignity, to stare at her, and leans on the desk*)

Excuse me. I'm an American and I get mixed up sometimes.

NICOLAS (*slowly*) No, but it is interesting. It bears out so much of what I have heard concerning your nation's strongly emotional tendencies towards parent worship. The fact, Miss Dagenham, that the guy is my father is of very minor importance. The essential fact is that he is Regent, and that his policy is leading my country into war.

MARY (*moving below the sofa*) That's what you think, I know. Anyway, it's what your Uncle Wilhelm thinks, your father thinks different. But you're only sixteen while he's—well, he told me forty, but I'll make a rough guess at forty-five. (*She turns and moves below the chair* LC) Isn't there just a chance that he might know better than you?

NICOLAS (*moving to the sofa and leaning over the back of it*) Now there is surely another American characteristic, no? The idea that the old are wise simply because they are not young, and that the young are children until they are twenty-one, but in America, I believe, they are children much longer.

MARY (*hotly*) Well, maybe, it's just because we're kinder and more clear-sighted than other people. (*She moves up* LC) We know that the most precious thing in life is childhood, and we don't see why we should take it away from people too soon. (*She moves to* L *of the table* C) Anyway, you mustn't argue with me on that subject. I'm prejudiced. I've never grown up, I admit, and I've never wanted to either, and if *I* think it's wrong for boys of sixteen to plot dirty tricks on their fathers, and try and shove them off into limbo, and then justify themselves by talking like they were George Bernard Shaw, well it's only me, see—(*she moves up* LC) and don't you go blaming my country just because of it.

(NICOLAS *smiles. There is a pause*)

NICOLAS. Miss Dagenham, may I pay you a compliment?
MARY (*suspiciously*) There'll be a catch to this, I'll bet.
NICOLAS (*simply*) Oh, no.
MARY. Go ahead, then.
NICOLAS (*simply*) I think I like you much the best of all my father's mistresses.

(*There is a pause*)

MARY (*at length*) Oh, er—well, er—anyway, I thank Your Majesty for the compliment. (*She curtsies and laughs*)

(LOUISA *enters down* L. *She carries a pack of playing cards*)

LOUISA (*crossing below the chair* LC *to* L *of the sofa*) I've found some cards. Let's play a game.
NICOLAS. Wouldn't you rather read your nice magazine?
LOUISA (*moving above the table* C) I've finished it. (*She shuffles the cards*) Let's play poker.
NICOLAS. I don't remember it well.
LOUISA. It's easy.
NICOLAS. What shall we play for?
LOUISA. Those chocolates. We'll each have twenty. (*She moves* R *of the chair* LC. *With an imperious gesture*) Miss Dagenham . . .
MARY (*loyally*) They belong to the Grand Duchess—ma'am. (*The salutation plainly sticks in her throat*)

(LOUISA *glares murderously at Mary*)

LOUISA (*after a pause; viciously*) I've never heard of Fifi. I don't believe there *is* such a play. (*She sits on the sofa at the left end. To Nicolas*) We'll play for money and remember what we lose.

(NICOLAS *moves round the end of the sofa and sits on it at the right end*)

MARY (*after a slight pause; to Nicolas*) Shall I help Your Majesty with your cards? (*She moves above the sofa and stands* C *of it, between Nicolas and Louisa*)
NICOLAS. Thank you. Most kind.

(LOUISA *deals five cards to Nicolas and herself*)

LOUISA (*to Nicolas*) How many cards?
MARY (*whispering to Nicolas*) Three.
NICOLAS (*discarding three cards*) Three.

(LOUISA *gives three cards to Nicolas*)

LOUISA (*discarding four cards*) I'm taking four.
MARY (*whispering to Nicolas*) That means she's only got an Ace or a King.
LOUISA. It doesn't mean anything of the kind. Now, you bet.
NICOLAS (*after whispered advice*) Sixpence.
LOUISA. I'll raise you a shilling.
NICOLAS (*after further whispered advice*) I'll raise you two shillings.
LOUISA (*after due thought*) I'll raise you a hundred pounds.
NICOLAS. You haven't got a hundred pounds.
LOUISA. I can get it. All right, then. (*She thinks*) I'll raise you a thousand Styrian marks.
MARY (*mildly*) Ma'am, I wonder whether you should . . . ?
LOUISA. Silence, please. Speak only when you are addressed. A thousand Styrian marks.

(MARY, *with pursed lips, nods quietly and whispers to Nicolas*)

NICOLAS (*at length*) Fifty thousand Carpathian crowns.

LOUISA (*rising*) A hundred thousand Styrian marks.
NICOLAS (*rising; without consultation*) Two hundred thousand Carpathian crowns.
LOUISA (*kneeling on the sofa*) Five hundred thousand Styrian marks.
NICOLAS (*kneeling on the sofa*) Nine hundred thousand . . .

(MARY *frantically tries to restrain Nicolas*)

MARY. Sir—I beg you . . .
LOUISA (*bouncing triumphantly on the sofa*) Yes, but he said it! He said it! A million Styrian marks.
MARY. I think we'd better see her. Say, "See you".
NICOLAS. See you.

(LOUISA *triumphantly lays down her cards*)

MARY. But that's only two pairs.
LOUISA. Well?
MARY. We have four Queens.
LOUISA. Two pairs is better.
MARY. No, it isn't. The King wins.
LOUISA (*loudly*) He doesn't. He doesn't. In Styria two pairs is better.
NICOLAS. Miss Dagenham is American and this is an American game.
LOUISA. It isn't. It's a Styrian game.
NICOLAS (*raising his voice*) It's an American game. Anyone knows that. Billy the Kid invented it.
LOUISA (*screaming*) My uncle invented it. It's a Styrian game.
MARY (*pacifically*) Really, ma'am, I think it really is an American game, you know, and in our rules, two pairs are definitely less than fours.
LOUISA (*rising and leaning forward; viciously*) Shall I tell you what you are? You're both of you dirty cheats. (*She throws her cards at Nicolas, then crosses down* L)
NICOLAS (*rising; furiously*) I will not be so insulted—(*he crosses to Louisa*) nor will Miss Dagenham. (*He pulls Louisa's hair*) Take that back at once.
LOUISA (*screaming*) I won't. I won't. I won't. Dirty cheats, dirty cheats, dirty cheats. Ow! You're hurting. Stop it! Dirty cheats!

(*The* FOOTMEN *open the double doors.*
The REGENT *enters by the double doors, a benign smile on his face. The smile is wiped off his face at what he sees*)

REGENT (*angrily*) Nicolas! What are you doing?

(*The* FOOTMEN *close the double doors.* NICOLAS *reluctantly releases Louisa, moves below the sofa and stands with his back to her.* MARY *moves to* R *of the chair* LC. *The* REGENT *moves to* L *of the chair* LC. LOUISA *flies to the Regent for protection, holding on to his left arm*)

THE SLEEPING PRINCE

LOUISA. Uncle Charles, I have to protest. Nicolas pulled my hair, Miss Dagenham was insolent, and both of them have obtained money from me at poker by what I can only call sharp practice.

REGENT. My dear Louisa, I am sure there is some little mistake . . .

LOUISA (*with dignity*) There is no mistake whatever. (*She moves to the table L and collects her hat and gloves*) As for the money, it will be paid in full, of course, by my father—(*she moves to the double doors*) although what observation he may have to make concerning the transaction I cannot say. I am now going to look for my mother. (*She opens the upstage half of the double doors. With a curtsy to Nicolas*) Your Majesty.

(LOUISA *exits. The* FOOTMAN *closes the door. The* REGENT *looks grimly from Mary to Nicolas*)

REGENT (*at length; to Nicolas*) How much?
NICOLAS (*muttering*) A million.
REGENT (*appalled*) A million?
MARY (*reassuringly*) Oh, not pounds. Only Styrian marks. (*Murmuring*) They're about three and a half to the dollar, aren't they? I don't know what that makes them to the pound. Let me see now . . .

REGENT (*to Nicolas*) This conduct is utterly appalling—worse even, and this is saying much, than I might have expected from you.

MARY. It was entirely her fault.
REGENT (*coldly*) Miss Dagenham, is it not time you were at your theatre?

MARY (*moving up* C) Not quite. I was here for the whole interview. The King did his best—and his best was a good deal better than mine would have been, let me tell you, considering the acute provocation he suffered from that little—(*she restrains herself*) Princess.

REGENT. I see you have found a champion, Nicolas. (*He crosses to L of Nicolas*) I wonder if Miss Dagenham can help you in another even more serious matter in which she is as deeply involved as yourself. The telephone operator reports that you talked to the German Ambassador this morning. That is so?

NICOLAS (*tensely*) Yes.
REGENT. After Miss Dagenham had obtained you the number?
NICOLAS. She didn't know what the number was.
REGENT. You passed some message, didn't you?
NICOLAS. Yes.
REGENT. About your forthcoming *coup d'état*.
NICOLAS. That exists only in your and your secret police's imagination, Father.
REGENT (*quietly menacing*) What exactly was the message?

NICOLAS. Your operator will tell you.
REGENT. She doesn't speak German.
NICOLAS. I know. I found that out.
REGENT (*after a pause; quietly*) Will you tell me that message, Nicky?
NICOLAS (*moving to* L *of the desk and looking towards the window*) Isn't it nice it was such a fine day for the Coronation?
REGENT (*after a pause*) You will go to your room. Colonel Hoffman will visit you there later.

(NICOLAS *shrugs his shoulders philosophically and crosses to the double doors*)

(*He moves to* L *of the table* R) And, of course, there is no question whatever of your going to the ball tonight. I prefer not to keep company with traitors.
NICOLAS (*bowing to Mary*) Miss Dagenham, I say this with sincerity. It has been a real pleasure.

(MARY *curtsies.*
NICOLAS *exits by the double doors. There is a long pause, during which* MARY *picks up the cards and puts them on the desk. The* REGENT *stands deep in thought. Finally he moves to the chair down* R *and sits wearily*)

REGENT (*more to himself than to Mary*) What am I to do with such a boy?
MARY (*moving in front of the Regent and looking down at him*) If you were asking me that question seriously, my darling, I'd answer you. But as you're not, I'll just take off all my finery— (*she crosses to* R *of the table* C) and slip quietly out of your life for ever.
REGENT (*angrily*) I *am* asking you—although, Herr Gott, I know what the answer's going to be. Something about his not having enough love in his life, I suppose?
MARY (*lightly*) Not such a bad guess.
REGENT (*even more angrily*) And Wolffstein, whom he's conspiring with, and the other more dangerous one to whom he sent the message today, and Kaiser Wilhelm who's only waiting for me to be eliminated and Nicky made King in order to start his war, and all those poor dupes of my fellow countrymen who are shooting at my policemen this evening, I suppose, all of *them* need more love in their lives, too?
MARY (*removing her pearls*) I shouldn't be at all surprised. (*She looks longingly at the pearls, and then, averting her eyes, puts them on the table* C)
REGENT (*at length*) Kreuz donner wetter noch mal! Such sentimental idiocy.
MARY. Why do you always swear in German? (*She removes her diamonds*)

REGENT. Because the Germans have the best oaths. (*He mutters unhappily*) And the best machine-guns.

MARY. Yes. I suppose, "Cross thunder weather yet again" wouldn't sound nearly so fierce. (*She holds the diamonds up to the light*) I often wondered what it *was* about diamonds. Now I know. (*With a sigh*) Oh, well! (*She averts her gaze and slips the necklace on to the table* C)

REGENT (*suddenly and sharply*) What?

MARY. I said I wondered what it was about diamonds...

REGENT. Before that. You translated—do you speak German?

MARY. Oh, yes.

REGENT (*excited*) Then you heard his message?

MARY. Oh, yes.

(*The* REGENT *rises and moves to* R *of the sofa*)

But I'm not going to tell you what it was, so don't excite yourself too much.

(*The* REGENT *stares menacingly at her*)

Gosh, you're pretty when you look fierce.

REGENT. Miss Dagenham, you are in possession of some very dangerous information, and I must warn you...

MARY. Now you can't put the thumbscrews on me, darling, and you know it.

REGENT (*after a pause; moving towards Mary*) Oh, my dear, dear child, if only you would understand...

MARY. And you can't wheedle me either.

(*There is a pause during which they stare at each other, then the* REGENT *turns away to* R *and stands with his back turned to her*)

REGENT (*suddenly*) Himmel heilige bimbaum! (*He moves behind the desk and turns*)

MARY. Well done. That's the best yet.

REGENT (*across the desk; pleadingly*) The peace of the entire world depends...

MARY. Oh, yes, I know. The *end* couldn't be better, but telling tales out of school and getting other people into trouble make bad *means*.

REGENT (*moving behind the desk chair*) But Herr Gott noch mal! The world isn't a nursery. It's a jungle. When you are surrounded by ravening lions, do you refuse to use violence because it is bad means?

MARY. Well, Daniel did all right, didn't he?

(*The* REGENT *opens his mouth to deliver an expletive*)

(*She crosses above the desk to the Regent*) Now, don't swear any more, my darling, or you'll run out of oaths. I'm not going to tell you, and that's flat. What I will tell you is I think your treatment of your son just now was not only bad means, but bad policy.

REGENT (*crossing below the desk and above the sofa to the table* C; *scornfully*) Good policy, I suppose, would be to kiss the little *schweinhund* on both cheeks, and say, "Let bygones be bygones, dear child, come to the ball"?

MARY (*leaning on the upstage corner of the window*) The words right out of my mouth. When one line of attack fails, switch to another. You should be an expert on those tactics. Remember last night.

(*The* REGENT *is about to swear again*)

(*She crosses to him*) Now, now. Just ask yourself this question, my darling. Who is Nicky more likely to tell his plot to—nasty old Colonel Hoffman, giving him what-for in his room, or his dream prince of a gorgeous father giving him a strawberry ice at a ball?

REGENT (*turning away; furiously*) Do not call me by these names. It is grotesque.

MARY. One day I may call you by other names; but for the moment, my darling, you'll have to excuse the language of love. (*She moves to* R *of the table* C *and picks up her bag*) Well, I'm ready for my good-bye kiss.

(*The* REGENT *moves to Mary, brusquely kisses her on the cheek, then rings the bell on the table* C)

Is that all I get?

REGENT. The way I am feeling at the moment, it is considerably too much.

(*The* FOOTMEN *open the double doors.*
The MAJOR-DOMO *enters*)

Tell His Majesty to come and see me.

(*The* MAJOR-DOMO *bows and exits. The* FOOTMEN *close the double doors. The* REGENT *moves up* LC)

MARY. What about my parting present?

(*The* REGENT *stares malevolently at Mary, then silently crosses above her to the desk, takes a box from the desk drawer, hands it to her and turns away*)

Oh, no, no. Pin it on, please.

(*The* REGENT *takes the brooch out of the box and pins it on*)

Now say what you said to me this morning.

REGENT. If I do you will only laugh, because my epaulettes are scratching you or something, and I shall be disconcerted again. (*He tosses the box on to the table* C)

MARY. Take the risk.

REGENT (*murmuring*) It has been wonderful knowing you. If only it could have lasted longer.
MARY. Thank you, my darling. (*She kisses him gently on the mouth*)

(*The* REGENT *responds. They disengage as the* FOOTMEN *open the double doors. The* REGENT *crosses down* R.
The MAJOR-DOMO *enters and stands above the doorway*)

MAJOR-DOMO (*announcing*) His Majesty.

(NICOLAS *enters by the double doors and stands silently by the doorway, staring defiantly at his father.*
The MAJOR-DOMO *exits, and the* FOOTMEN *close the doors*)

REGENT (*quietly*) Nicky—sit down, Nicky——

(NICOLAS *crosses to the chair* LC *and sits*)

—this German Embassy affair has made me most unhappy.

(*A look passes between* MARY *and the* REGENT)

(*He walks up* C *and down*) I have always known that you and I did not see eye to eye on policy——

(MARY *crosses to the desk, looking for her raincoat*)

—but that my own son should conspire against me has been a most bitter shock.
NICOLAS. I don't see why it should be. You told me last night that your secret police . . .
REGENT (*moving to the sofa and sitting in an attitude of despair*) I was joking, of course. Ah, Nicky, Nicky! I don't know whether you realize how easy it is to break a father's heart.

(MARY *moves behind the chair* LC, *watches this exchange interestedly, then surreptitiously shows the* REGENT *an attitude more indicative of heartbreak. He adopts it*)

NICOLAS (*at length*) If you mean *your* heart, Father, I don't.
REGENT. Ah, perhaps that is because I don't wear my heart on my sleeve, Nicky. Some people prefer to keep their feelings bottled up, and I, it may be . . .
MARY (*in an apologetic murmur*) Er—sorry to interrupt—but have you seen an old raincoat lying around anywhere?
REGENT (*bewildered*) An old raincoat?
MARY. Yes. (*She remembers and sees the raincoat behind the chair* L) Oh, I remember. (*She moves to the chair* L *and picks up the raincoat*) Here it is. I don't want to be seen going through the stage door in an evening dress, you see. It looks too silly. So sorry. Go on. (*She puts on the raincoat*)

(*The* REGENT *sits, trying to recover his flow of thought*)

REGENT. Anyway, Nicky, I don't want to say any more about it, tonight.

(*A look passes between* MARY *and the* REGENT)

I have decided to let bygones be bygones. In spite of everything you may come to the ball.

NICOLAS. Thank you, Father, but I don't think I want to. I think I'd rather go to bed.

MARY (*moving to* L *of Nicolas; shocked*) Oh, but you must go, sir. I mean, just think—the greatest ball of the season—wonderful dresses, beautiful uniforms, the decorations alone costing five thousand pounds——

NICOLAS. No.

MARY. —invitations harder to get than . . .

NICOLAS. No. I would have liked to, but stepmother says she's not going because she's tired, and I won't know anyone, and I won't have anyone to dance with.

(MARY *moves to the double doors*)

REGENT (*crossly*) Well, then, invite someone to dance with.

NICOLAS. Invite someone?

REGENT. Yes. I can easily arrange it.

NICOLAS. You mean—anyone?

REGENT. Yes. Anyone.

NICOLAS. All right, then. (*He rises and moves above the chair* LC) Miss Dagenham, will you accompany me to the ball at the Foreign Office tonight?

(*There is a long pause, while* MARY *looks over Nicolas' head and at the Regent's face*)

MARY (*at length*) I shall be most happy to obey Your Majesty's command.

NICOLAS. Oh, that's good.

(MARY *glances once more at the* REGENT, *whose face is expressionless, and wanders to the table* C, *picks up the jewels and shows them to Nicolas*)

MARY (*to Nicolas*) Do you think your stepmother will mind?

NICOLAS (*moving to* L *of the table* C; *excitedly*) Oh, no, of course not. She'll just say "What fun". And I'll borrow one of her tiaras for you, too.

MARY. Well—if they're going to see me leave the theatre in a tiara—(*she removes her raincoat, crosses, puts the raincoat behind the chair down* L, *then moves to* L *of the chair* LC) they can damn well see me arrive in evening dress.

NICOLAS (*moving between the sofa and the chair* LC) I think I shall find you another Order. The one you are wearing is not first class.

MARY. No? (*She looks at the Regent*) Oh well—I wasn't going to say anything, mind you, but if you feel that . . .

NICOLAS (*moving above the chair LC to Mary*) Then, I shall come in person to collect you at your theatre at eleven o'clock? (*He moves to the double doors*)

MARY. Yes, that'll be nice.

(*The* REGENT *sits, silent and grim-faced*)

(*She crosses to the Regent, unfastens her brooch and hands it to him, then moves to the table* C, *puts the jewellery in her handbag and backs to the double doors. In a small voice*) Well—see you later, then.

MARY *exits by the double doors as*—

the CURTAIN *falls*

SCENE 2

SCENE—*The same. About twelve-thirty the same night.*

When the CURTAIN *rises, a buffet table with supper is set up* C. *On the table* C *there is a large salver with two ice-buckets containing a bottle of champagne and a bottle of vodka, along with two vodka glasses. The* REGENT *is standing at the window. The* BUTLER *is standing at the table* C. *He takes the champagne out of the bucket, crosses to the* REGENT *who looks at it, then the* BUTLER *crosses and replaces the bottle. He then draws the cork of the vodka bottle.* PETER *enters by the double doors. The* BUTLER *bows and exits by the double doors, closing them after him.*

PETER (*crossing to* LC) I have to report, sir, that His Majesty has returned.

REGENT. Alone?

PETER. I fear not, sir.

REGENT (*crossing to* R *of Peter; alarmed*) She is here—in the Legation?

(PETER *nods*)

Where are they?

PETER. In the stewards' room.

REGENT. The stewards' room? What are they doing in the stewards' room?

PETER. There is a gramophone there. She is teaching him an American dance called the fox trot.

REGENT (*moving* C) Herr Gott noch mal!

PETER. Exactly, sir.

REGENT. But how did they travel from the ball? Why was his carriage sent away? What conveyance did they use?

PETER (*after a pause; in a shocked murmur*) A bus.
REGENT (*turning*) A bus? A *public* bus?
PETER. A number fifty-seven.
REGENT. But, in the name of Saint Francis, why?
PETER. It appears that His Majesty expressed a wish to travel in that manner.

(*There is a pause*)

REGENT (*moving to L of the sofa*) The girl's influence, I have no doubt.
PETER. Nor indeed, sir, have I.
REGENT (*sitting on the sofa*) This may mean a scandal, Northbrook.
PETER (*moving to L of the Regent*) I need hardly tell Your Royal Highness that all possible steps will be taken to dissuade the more responsible journals from reporting the occurrence. I cannot, of course, answer for the halfpenny press.
REGENT. Why did they leave the ball so soon, in any case?
PETER. I understand that Miss Dagenham, when dancing a two-step with His Majesty decided to—er—alter the tempo.
REGENT. You mean—a one-step?

(PETER *nods*)

At the Foreign Office?
PETER. I'm afraid so, sir.
REGENT. They were asked to leave the floor, of course?
PETER (*reassuringly*) Oh, no, sir. His Majesty, of course, was known. It was merely suggested to them that they should well—alter the tempo back again. However, the King thereupon expressed himself insulted and there were unfortunate words.
REGENT (*rising and moving up R*) Verflucht! I should never have left them out of my sight for a moment.
PETER (*reprovingly*) No, sir.
REGENT (*after a pause; distractedly*) Lucy Maidenhead is late.
PETER. Only a few minutes, sir.
REGENT. Her unpunctuality used to be one of her most irritating characteristics. I had hoped she might have grown out of it, by now. (*He crosses to R of Peter*) She has had, after all, time. (*He sits on the sofa at the right end*)
PETER (*moving to L of the table C*) I can venture to reassure Your Royal Highness that Lady Maidenhead hardly looks a day older than she did ten years ago. In fact, I think I can say that she seems to have found the secret of perpetual youth.
REGENT. I am most glad to hear it. (*Murmuring*) She must need it by now.
PETER (*moving above the sofa; concerned*) Oh dear! Is Your Royal Highness not feeling quite so enthusiastic about this reunion as

you did this morning? Should I meet the lady downstairs and make your excuses?
REGENT. No, no. Of course not. I am most looking forward to seeing Lucy again. Dear Lucy. Dear, enchanting, witty, grown-up Lucy . . .

(*The words die on the* REGENT'S *lips as the double doors are opened, unguarded for the moment by footmen, and* MARY *enters. She is looking very splendid and glittering in her tiara, Orders and jewels. The* REGENT *rises*)

MARY. Hullo.
REGENT. Hullo.
MARY (*moving to the buffet*) Oo! Oh, supper! How lovely. (*She moves to* L *of the sofa*) Oh, darling, how thoughtful of you.
REGENT (*at length*) Not at all.
MARY. I'll just nip down and say good night to Nicky, and then I'll be right back.

(MARY *exits by the double doors. The* REGENT *gives Peter a gloomy glance. There is a pause. The* REGENT *sits on the sofa at the right end*)

PETER (*encouragingly*) Come, come, sir. (*He moves to* R *of the sofa*) All that is needed is a little firmness. You should tell her straight out that the supper is not for her, and that you are expecting another guest.
REGENT. That is your considered suggestion for surmounting this crisis, Northbrook?
PETER. Yes, sir. It is.
REGENT (*savagely*) Then I can only say that I now fully understand why the Foreign Office always makes such a mess of its relations with the State Department. Northbrook—we are not here dealing with a civilized adult—but an unruly child. (*Roaring*) Do you think I am anxious to have supper for *three*?
PETER. I'm sorry, sir. I had not, I agree, considered that aspect. (*He crosses well down below the sofa to* L *of the Regent. After reflection*) The best policy, then, would appear to be for me to intercept Lady Maidenhead on arrival, and escort her to one of the downstairs rooms. There I can arrange to have another table laid . . .
REGENT. *Two* suppers I am to eat?
PETER. I'm afraid I see no alternative.
REGENT (*gloomily*) But how am I to leave this one? That is the crux, Northbrook.
PETER (*moving a step or two up* LC) A few moments after Lady Maidenhead arrives I shall come up and announce that the Minister urgently requires your presence in the Chancery, and that your business will last for at least an hour. You then say goodbye to Miss Dagenham—I shall be here, sir—no harm will come to you—and leave Miss Dagenham for me to escort to her home.

REGENT. "At least an hour" is hopeless. You had better say all night. Only so will your plans have the faintest chance of success.

(MARY *enters by the double doors and moves to* L *of the chair* LC. *She carries her handbag*)

MARY (*brightly*) Well, here I am. What a sweet little boy that is.
REGENT (*to Peter*) You may leave us, Northbrook.
PETER. Very well, sir.

(PETER, *after exchanging a meaning glance with* the REGENT, *backs out of the double doors*. MARY *moves below the table* C *and watches Peter go*)

MARY. Say! He doesn't do that half as well as me.
REGENT. Who is a sweet little boy? My son?
MARY. Yes. Far too grown-up for his age, of course, but I expect that's just the fault of his upbringing. (*She picks up the bottle of vodka and a glass and moves to* L *of the Regent*) Vodka?
REGENT. Thank you.

(MARY *pours a very generous measure*)

Stop. That is too much.
MARY (*handing the glass to the Regent*) Oh, you can take *that* all right, surely.

(*The* REGENT *swallows his drink at a gulp*)

Hey. That's too quick. I wanted to give you a toast. (*She takes the glass from him and refills it*) You'll have to have another now.
REGENT. Not so much, please. (*He snatches the glass from her*)
MARY. Say, you don't want to spoil my illusions of you, do you?
REGENT. What are your illusions of me?
MARY (*moving to the table* C *and pouring an infinitesimal portion of vodka into a glass for herself*) Well, your capacity for vodka is certainly one of them. (*She puts the bottle on the table and raises her glass*) Here's to more love in everybody's life.
REGENT (*muttering*) Cheerioh! (*He swallows his drink at a gulp, without visible effect*)

(MARY *drains her glass, then puts it on the table* C, *moves to the sofa, sits on it,* L *of the Regent, and takes a document from her handbag*)

MARY (*very business-like*) Well, now, I have a little document here that I think will interest you. The writing's bad, because I did it on the top of a bus, so I'll read it to you. Incidentally, that poor little creature has never been on top of a bus in his life. Imagine. It was a bigger thrill for him than going to the ball was for me, and that's saying something. Now. (*She reads*) "Manifesto to my faithful subjects. I, Nicolas the Eighth, King, do hereby renounce and reject utterly the overtures lately made to me by certain persons that I should assume the powers of government before the appointed time, and I do hereby solemnly adjure all citizens of the realm to unite loyally and wholeheartedly under the Regency of my father, the Grand Duke Charles, for the settled peace of the Kingdom. Signed—Nicolas."

(*The* REGENT *snatches the document from her and looks at it*)

REGENT. But it isn't signed Nicolas at all.

(MARY *takes a crumpled piece of paper from her bag, rises, crosses to the chair* LC *and sits on it*)

MARY. No. Not yet, but it will be. There's got to be a little give and take in this life, you know, darling. You have something to sign, too. (*She indicates the paper*) These are Nicky's conditions.

REGENT (*furiously*) Conditions?

MARY. Oh, they're very simple ones. I took them down just as he said them. This is a bit of a scrawl, too. We were sitting on the stairs leading to the ballroom and people kept treading on us. Incidentally, did you know that a one-step at a Court Ball is about as popular as a fan dance at a church fête? Idiotic. (*She reads*) "One. Martial law must not be declared. Two. The King must be allowed to purchase a new motor bicycle and to ride it anywhere in his dominion without let or hindrance. Three. There must be a general amnesty of all political prisoners, Parliament must be dissolved forthwith ,and a general election called. Four. The marriage between the King and the Princess Louisa will definitely *not* take place." That's all.

(*There is a pause. The* REGENT, *with a grim expression, rises, crosses to the table* C *and absently pours himself another vodka*)

(*Approvingly*) Quite right, my darling. That'll help you to see it all in the best possible light.

(*The* REGENT *swallows his drink at a gulp and puts the glass on the table* C)

REGENT (*at length*) Herr Gott kreuz donner-wetter noch mal!

MARY. Funny. That's just what I thought you'd say.

REGENT (*crossing to* L *of the desk*) You two have been having a fine joke at my expense this evening.

MARY (*hurt*) That isn't true, darling. I've worked, as hard as I know, *for* you tonight, not against you. I've got all the details of his plot now, you know, and I really think it would have succeeded. Or may succeed yet, if you're foolish enough not to sign this bit of paper.

REGENT (*leaning on the desk*) What does it matter, either way? Declaring a general election will put the German party in power as surely as his coup d'état ...

MARY. Oh, I don't know. After all, you might win. You know,

that's the funny thing about general elections. You never can tell who's going to win. Now, if you could only beat Mr Wolffstein constitutionally...

REGENT (*scornfully*) Huh! (*He moves to* R *of the sofa*) Beat Mr Wolffstein constitutionally! Beat Mr Wolffstein—constitutionally... (*His voice trails away as an idea seems to come to him and he looks at the document*)

MARY (*virtuously*) Yes, and wouldn't that take the wax out of the Kaiser's moustache!

REGENT (*flourishing the document; abruptly*) Did you phrase this?

MARY (*innocently*) I think so. Why?

REGENT (*glowering at her*) Herr Gott! How could you have so deceived me!

MARY. Deceived you, darling? What are you talking about?

REGENT (*angrily*) A brilliant intrigante.

MARY. I don't know what that is, but I do hope it's not as rude as it sounds.

REGENT (*moving up* C; *incredulously*) Of course you do not realize what you are making the boy sign?

MARY. Yes, dear. A manifesto.

REGENT (*moving up* LC; *excitedly*) A confession. An abject confession by my son that the leaders of the German party had been plotting with him to overthrow me, and what is much more important, to destroy the Constitution. (*He quotes*) "The overtures lately made to me by certain persons." Ausgezeichnet! (*He chuckles and moves to* L *of the chair* LC) Don't you see what I can do now?

(MARY *shakes her head*)

(*He moves in front of Mary*) My dear child, do you not see? Now it is I and not Wolffstein who can go to the country as the champion of freedom, of the Constitution and of democracy. (*He moves below the sofa. Happily*) You know, with this in my hands, it might even not be necessary to rig a single election.

MARY. I should just hope not indeed. (*She rises and moves below the table* C) Oh, but darling, how clever of you to see all that in that! Have another vodka.

REGENT. What? No, I have had enough.

MARY (*refilling his glass*) Oh, just a little one. (*She moves to the Regent and hands him the glass*) Don't you want to eat?

REGENT (*crossing and sitting in the chair* LC) No, I'm not hungry.

(MARY *crosses slowly to the table* L)

Of course, the timing of events will have to be most carefully considered. I hold the initiative now.

(MARY *switches out the lamp on the table* L)

I must not lose it.

MARY (*moving down* L) Oh, but I'm sure that with your fine brain and your great flair for politics and your wonderful grasp of a situation, you wouldn't ever lose a thing like an initiative. (*She kicks the footstool from down* L *towards the chair* LC, *then sits on the stool*) Oh, I do envy you, darling.

REGENT. Envy me?

MARY. For being blessed with so much. Rank, position, wealth, looks—oh, such wonderful, wonderful looks—youth . . .

REGENT. You are flattering.

MARY (*rising, perching herself on the left arm of the chair* LC *and putting her arm around the Regent's shoulders*) Oh, no. After all, forty is still young. And above all, virility and strength of character. (*She pauses*) Wouldn't you be more comfortable with your feet up? (*She points to the sofa*)

REGENT (*still abstracted*) No, thank you.

MARY. Another vodka?

REGENT. No, thank you. (*He suddenly leaps up*) Herr Gott, I have it.

MARY (*startled*) What?

REGENT (*crossing down* R) I shall release Wolffstein. Tomorrow night on my return I shall release them all, unconditionally. That will confuse them utterly. (*He moves to* L *of the desk*) They will think I have done it from weakness.

MARY (*rising and moving up* C) Wonderful.

REGENT (*moving up* RC) Yes, but here lies the real *clou* of the plan. The very next day while they are off guard, rejoicing in their apparent victory, I shall suddenly dissolve Parliament, call an immediate general election and publish in every newspaper in the kingdom the King's manifesto——

(MARY *moves to the table* C *and refills the Regent's glass*)

—with appropriate editorial comment—I shall have, of course, to work hard there—these editors are such *dumkopfs*—but happily I compose such things without great difficulty. (*He leans against the back of the sofa*) The effect in the country will be immense. Immense.

(MARY *moves to the* REGENT *and hand him the drink, which he absently throws back*)

MARY (*with breathless admiration*) Brilliant. Quite, quite brilliant. And all out of that little piece of paper in your hand.

REGENT (*handing the glass to Mary*) Yes, I am most happy with this thought of mine. Most happy. (*He crosses to the desk, puts the document on it, then sits, rather heavily, on the sofa*)

MARY (*putting the glass on the table* C) And so you should be, my darling. I can see you haven't earned the title of the Fox of the Balkans for nothing.

REGENT. Am I called so?

MARY. Didn't you know?
REGENT (*pleased*) The Fox of the Balkans. Hm!
MARY. And those eyebrows make you look rather like a fox, too. (*She sits on the sofa,* L *of the Regent*) A beautiful, sleek, dangerous animal. But such a lonely one.
REGENT (*with a sigh*) Oh, my child. It is my lot to be lonely. (*He rests his head on the back of the sofa and affectionately pats her cheek*)
MARY. Must it always be? (*She reaches out and presses the bell on the table*)
REGENT. Ah yes. It must. It must. (*He strokes her hair*) Dear child——

(*The music of a violin, playing a waltz, can be heard off*)

—if only you could understand . . . (*He suddenly sits bolt upright*) Where's that music coming from?
MARY. It's that Hungarian again, I expect. You told me he played every night.
REGENT. Yes, but . . . (*He stares suspiciously at her*)
MARY. Never mind, my darling. Go on about being lonely. (*She pushes him gently back, and rests her head lovingly on his chest*) Have you never loved?
REGENT. I have never allowed myself to love. Love is the enemy of all the cold, hard virtues that a man must have to rule a country such as mine.
MARY. Who says so?
REGENT. Caesar Augustus was the first.
MARY. And what happened to him?
REGENT. He became the ruler of the world.
MARY. Poor lamb.
REGENT. You think he needed love in his life?
MARY. Like crazy he did.
REGENT. As much as I?
MARY. I don't know. That's hard to judge. (*Gently*) You see, *I* wasn't there to provide it for him. (*She kisses him*)
REGENT (*after a pause; gently*) Do you wish to catch your fox in a net?
MARY. Oh, but it would be such a very soft little net—made of the very finest spun cobwebs. (*She raises her head to look at him*)

(*The* REGENT *pulls Mary to him and kisses her*)

REGENT (*at length*) Ah, but even a net of the very spinest-fun —the sfinest-pun . . . (*He sits up, surprised*) Herr Gott! I am drunk.
MARY (*concerned*) Oh, no, you're not, are you, darling? Look, just get up and see if you can walk all right. (*She points vaguely towards the door down* L) Walk to that door, for instance.

(*The* REGENT *rises and walks fairly steadily to the door down* L)

All right, come back.

(*The* REGENT *returns to the sofa and half kneels on it, leaning over her*)
There you see. Now go on with what you were saying.
REGENT. Ah, but what are words when deeds can say so much more?
MARY. Oh, no, darling, not again. Can't you think of anything else to say?
REGENT (*at length; feelingly*) Draga kis galambom gyere ide, maradj itten, szeress engem ahogy en szeretlek teged.
MARY. Oh, excuse me, darling, I didn't quite catch what you said.
REGENT (*at length*) I love you.
MARY. I love you. Oh gosh, Your Royal Highness, how I love you. (*She kisses him*)

(*The* REGENT *responds. The music grows louder.*
PETER *enters suddenly by the double doors. The* REGENT *rises and moves hurriedly* R)

PETER (*briskly*) Sir, you are most urgently required in the Chancery...
REGENT (*crossing below Mary and advancing on Peter*) Northbrook! These constant intrusions of yours are beyond all bounds. How dare you!

PETER ⎫
     ⎬ (*together*) ⎧ But, Your Royal Highness—(*meaningly*) the *Minister* has arrived—(*he backs hastily to the double doors*) if you see what I mean...
REGENT ⎭   ⎩ Will you please not argue with me. Leave the room at once—and think yourself lucky I am not telephoning to the Foreign Secretary immediately...

PETER *backs hastily out by the double doors, closing them after him.*
MARY *suddenly laughs, and the* REGENT *laughs with her. Their laughter dies and they look lovingly at each other, as—*

the CURTAIN *falls*

SCENE 3

SCENE—*The same. 10 a.m. the following morning.*

When the CURTAIN *rises, the table* C *is set with coffee for two. The double doors stand open. The* MAJOR-DOMO *and the* BUTLER *are standing talking up* C. PETER *enters by the double doors. He is still in diplomatic uniform and indeed, from his agitated manner, it would seem doubtful if he has taken it off since the night before. He moves down*

C. *The* MAJOR-DOMO *moves to* R *of Peter, and they begin a whispered conversation, circling the sofa as they talk. The* MAJOR-DOMO *whispers his replies to Peter's questions, each one of which seems to disturb* PETER *deeply. They occasionally glance at the door down* R. *Having circled, the* MAJOR-DOMO *finishes* L *of Peter. The* MAJOR-DOMO *speaks in German and* PETER *gives him a look, then the* MAJOR-DOMO *and the* BUTLER *exit by the double doors, which are closed by the* FOOTMEN. PETER, *nervously gnawing his knuckles, is alone for a moment.* NICOLAS *enters down* R. *He is dressed in a plain suit and looks rather bewildered.*

NICOLAS (*crossing to* R *of Peter below the sofa*) Mr Northbrook, is my father quite well this morning?
PETER. I gather so, sir.
NICOLAS (*in a stunned voice*) He has just—embraced me.
PETER. Well—surely he has done that often before?
NICOLAS. In public, of course. But this was in private, Mr Northbrook, in his bedroom with only his valets to see it. And he called me his darling boy.
PETER. How nice.
NICOLAS. It is most suspicious. He was asking, too, the most extraordinary, not to say embarrassing questions.

(PETER *looks blankly at Nicolas*)

Was I not sometimes very lonely, had he always been a good father to me, did I not feel the lack of love in my life? (*He assumes from Peter's blank expression that he has not heard*) Mr Northbrook, my father asked if I did not feel the lack of *love* in my life?
PETER. Yes, sir. I heard you.
NICOLAS. You are not surprised? You have heard something already perhaps. Was the excitement yesterday too much for him? Is there cause for concern?
PETER. No, sir. At least not regarding his health.
NICOLAS (*darkly*) I strongly suspect some Foreign Office hocus-pocus in all this. (*He moves* R *a little*)
PETER (*moving to* L *of the table* C; *stiffly*) The Foreign Office, sir, never resorts to hocus-pocus. You are doubtless thinking of the Quai d'Orsay.

(*The* REGENT *enters down* R *and crosses to* R *of Peter. He is wearing a dressing-gown and is plainly in a sunny mood*)

REGENT. Ah, good morning, Northbrook. Punctual as usual, I see. Splendid. Herr Gott! How handsome you look in that uniform of yours. I had meant to tell you that last night, but it somehow slipped my mind. (*He pours himself a cup of coffee*) Nicky—my darling boy.
NICOLAS. Yes, Father?
REGENT (*picking up his coffee, crossing and sitting in the chair* LC)

Nothing. Just my darling boy. (*He smiles affectionately at Nicolas*) You had better get ready. We leave in ten minutes.

NICOLAS (*crossing above the sofa towards the double doors*) Yes, Father.

REGENT. Give me a kiss, Nicky.

NICOLAS (*stopping; appalled*) Another kiss?

REGENT. Why not?

NICOLAS. One can overdo such things.

REGENT. Nonsense. Fathers *should* kiss their sons.

NICOLAS. When they are children, but not when . . .

REGENT (*sharply*) Nicky! Come and give me a kiss, this instant.

(NICOLAS *shrugs his shoulders, moves to* R *of the Regent and awkwardly pecks his father's cheek. Then he shrugs his shoulders at Peter, behind the Regent's back, and exits by the double doors, which are closed by the* FOOTMEN. PETER *moves to* R *of the Regent*)

(*He leans back in his chair and beams at Peter*) Well, well, Northbrook. Well, well, well.

PETER. Well, well, indeed, sir.

REGENT. A wonderful morning, is it not?

PETER. Yes, sir. Wonderful. (*He takes a letter from his pocket*) I have here a letter for Your Royal Highness of a somewhat private nature. (*He hands the letter to the Regent*)

REGENT. Who is it from?

PETER. Lady Maidenhead.

REGENT (*handing his cup to Peter*) Oh. (*He opens the letter, and his face darkens slightly as he reads*) Dear, dear! Oh, well. (*He tears the letter up. Thoughtfully*) You know, Northbrook, what I think is the trouble with Lady Maidenhead?

PETER (*politely*) She has not enough love in her life?

REGENT (*taking the cup from Peter*) Too much. (*He puts the pieces of the letter in the saucer*) One should keep a balance in these things. (*He finishes his coffee, hands the cup to Peter, then rises and crosses to* R) Now, Northbrook, I have one or two commissions for you—to be performed after we leave.

PETER (*putting the cup on the table* C) I shall be honoured.

REGENT (*moving up* RC) First, a *laisser-passer* must be obtained for a journey to Carpathia in a few days' time, and made out in the name of Miss Mary Morgan.

PETER (*alarmed*) Miss Who?

REGENT (*moving above the sofa*) Citizeness of the United State profession—actress—stage name, Elaine Dagenham.

PETER (*almost relieved*) Oh. I was beginning to wonder, sir.

REGENT (*moving round the desk to the window*) Second—for the journey itself, a special coach must be attached to the Orient Express for the accommodation of Miss Morgan and her staff.

PETER. Her staff?

REGENT. Well, her habilleuse, or whatever . . .

PETER. Yes, sir. The expense of course to be charged to Your Royal Highness?

REGENT (*crossly*) I should have supposed that the British Government might afford so trifling an outlay, in view of the importance of Miss Dagenham's mission.

PETER (*politely*) I shall apply to the Chancellor of the Exchequer in person, sir, but I am just a shade on the doubtful side whether . . .

REGENT (*impatiently*) No matter, no matter. Enough of this cheeseparing. (*He moves below the desk then up* C) Special servants must, of course, be engaged for the journey, and I shall send one of my own chefs to board the train at Ostend. Flowers, bowers of flowers, in the saloons and bedrooms, of course—roses, I believe, are her favourites—(*he moves down* LC *and stands behind the chair*) and champagne, vodka, caviare—you will attend to these petty details, yourself, will you not?

PETER (*with a sigh*) I shall be overjoyed, sir.

REGENT (*leaning over the back of the chair*) Now, one other little matter. She may require a few dresses, furs and personal ornaments for the journey. You will see to it that in that respect she is given *carte blanche*.

PETER (*after a slight pause*) *Carte* quite *blanche*, sir?

REGENT (*moving up* L) As *blanche* as she cares to make it. (*He crosses up* R) I have, you see, Northbrook—in your idiom—got it bad.

PETER (*with a sigh*) You have indeed, sir.

REGENT. It is a strange phenomenon. (*He moves above the sofa*) I do not yet quite know how it has happened to me. For forty-three years I have tried . . . (*Excitedly*) There, you see, Northbrook. I now even state my age correctly. (*Wearily*) Herr Gott noch mal! There is something in this falling in love that frightens me.

PETER. I am not surprised, sir. I have myself always studiously avoided the ailment.

REGENT. Take care, Northbrook. Take care. There is a nemesis for such as you—and it may well, one day, take some such form as a Circassian trapeze artist in a music-hall at Casablanca. (*He crosses to the door down* R) And when it does, Northbrook—when it does—you, too, will awake from the long grey sleep of Prudence to the magnificent scarlet dawn of Folly. (*He opens the door. He seems extremely taken aback at what he has just said*) Um Gottes willen! That was myself speaking?

PETER. It was, sir.

REGENT (*after a pause; with a deep sigh*) Oh well, I suppose it cannot be helped.

(*The* REGENT *philosophically shrugs his shoulders, then exits down* R. PETER *crosses to the desk and sits. There is a slight pause.*

NICOLAS *furtively puts his head round the upstage half of the double doors. He carries a small jewel case and a photograph.* PETER *rises and crosses to* R *of the table* C)

NICOLAS. My father is here?
PETER. Just gone into his room, sir.
NICOLAS (*crossing quickly to* L *of Peter*) Thank heavens! (*He hands the case and photograph to Peter*) I want you, if you see Miss Dagenham, to say good-bye to her for me, and give her this small parting present. Also this photograph.
PETER. Most certainly, sir.
NICOLAS (*hurriedly*) Tell her I enjoyed myself last night more than I ever have before in my life, and thank her most gratefully.
PETER. I shall indeed, sir.

(NICOLAS *looks furtively at the door down* R, *then goes quickly to the double doors.* PETER *crosses to the desk*)

NICOLAS. Has he kissed you, too?
PETER. Not yet, sir. (*He puts the case and photograph on the desk*)
NICOLAS. I should not be too confident, Mr Northbrook. Do you know that I have never been so scared of him in my whole life as this morning. It is all most disconcerting.

(NICOLAS *exits by the double doors.* PETER, *left alone, crosses to the table* C, *prudently picks up the scraps of Lady Maidenhead's letter, places them in an ashtray, and puts a match to them.*
MARY *enters down* L. *She has on the same evening dress, stripped now of all ornaments*)

MARY (*crossing to the window*) Playing with fire?
PETER. What? Oh, good morning, Miss Dagenham. Yes, I am.
MARY. Good morning. That's a sport you should leave to me. (*She looks out of the window*) Oh, what a lovely morning.
PETER (*moving to* R *of the table* C) Yes. Isn't it? (*He crosses to the desk and picks up the jewel case and photograph*) I have to present these to you, with His Majesty's compliments, and his thanks for last night, which he claims was the pleasantest evening he has ever spent in his life. (*He hands her the case and photograph*)
MARY. Gee! (*She looks at the photograph*) Gee, signed, too. How sweet of him. (*She opens the case*) Oh, a brooch with the royal arms. Wouldn't you have known it?

(*The double doors are opened by the* FOOTMEN.
The GRAND DUCHESS, *the* COUNTESS *and the* BARONESS *enter by the double doors. All are dressed in travelling clothes.* PETER *turns and crosses below the sofa to* LC. MARY *moves below the desk*)

GRAND DUCHESS (*moving down* C) Good morning, Mr Northbrook.

(*The* COUNTESS *crosses and stands up* R. *The* BARONESS *stands up* L)

PETER (*with a bow*) Your Imperial and Royal Highness. (*He backs and stands down* L)

GRAND DUCHESS. And Miss Dagenham. So delightful. How are you this morning?

MARY (*murmuring*) Very well, thank you, ma'am.

GRAND DUCHESS (*sitting on the chair* LC) My dear—such a night. Not a wink of sleep. Some dreadful drunkard fiddling in the corridor for hours and hours. And the night before, too, but not so long. I didn't dare go out to stop him, in case it was an anarchist, or a republican or something. One never knows nowadays, so disturbing. My dear, why do you always wear white?

MARY. Well—I suppose because I think it suits me, ma'am.

GRAND DUCHESS. But not *all* the time, dear. You are imitating the divine Sarah, no doubt, but even she, I am told, changes her dress occasionally. (*She looks* L) Maud. (*Crossly*) Where is that . . . ?

(*The* COUNTESS *hastily lowers her handkerchief from her nose and moves to* R *of the Grand Duchess*)

COUNTESS (*hastily*) Here, ma'am.

GRAND DUCHESS (*amazed*) Your cold has come *back* again, Maud?

COUNTESS. It appears to have, ma'am.

GRAND DUCHESS. I cannot possibly see how it could have done. Are you sure you are not imagining it?

COUNTESS. Quite sure, ma'am.

GRAND DUCHESS. Then there is no alternative but for me to prepare you one of my hot plasters.

COUNTESS (*involuntarily*) Oh, no, ma'am.

GRAND DUCHESS (*to Mary*) Most tedious. All those ingredients —and boiling everything—but happily it can all be done on the train. Did you say something, Maud?

COUNTESS. Most good of you, ma'am. It's just that it sometimes seems to burn a little.

GRAND DUCHESS. Burn? Of course it burns. That is its point, my dear. It burns the cold clean out of the body. Now what was it I called you for, dear? I remember. The present for Miss Dagenham.

COUNTESS (*opening her bag*) Yes, ma'am. I have it here. (*She takes a small jewel case from her bag and hands it to the Grand Duchess*)

GRAND DUCHESS. Good. (*To Mary*) Come here, dear.

(MARY *crosses to* R *of the Grand Duchess*)

Here is a little brooch for you, with the Carpathian arms on it. (*She hands the case to Mary*)

MARY. Ma'am, I am overwhelmed.

GRAND DUCHESS. And I have a photograph for you, too.

(*The* BARONESS *moves to* L *of the Grand Duchess and hands her a photograph, then retires up* L. *The* COUNTESS *retires up* R)

Let me see. Yes, I have signed it. (*She hands the photograph to Mary*) It goes best in a simple frame—nothing elaborate—I loathe elaborate frames—just plain gold—or even silver—not below eye level because, as you see, I am looking down and it would spoil the effect.

MARY. No, ma'am. Thank you very much indeed.

GRAND DUCHESS (*extending her cheek*) You may kiss me.

(MARY *kisses the Grand Duchess on her cheek, and curtsies at the same time, no mean feat*)

You already have a photograph, have you not, Mr Northbrook?

(MARY *crosses to the desk and puts the cases and photographs on it*)

PETER. Most proudly displayed, ma'am.

GRAND DUCHESS (*sharply*) Not on the same table as Olga Bosnia, I trust.

PETER. No, ma'am. I was most particular in obeying your instructions on that point.

(*The* REGENT *enters down* R. *He is now dressed in travelling clothes. He crosses to* R *of the sofa*)

GRAND DUCHESS (*rising*) My dear—(*she points to Mary*) look who has come to see us off.

REGENT. How delightful.

GRAND DUCHESS. So good of her to be here so early.

REGENT. Yes, indeed.

GRAND DUCHESS (*moving between the sofa and chair* LC) You will be at the station, Mr Northbrook?

PETER. Of course, ma'am.

GRAND DUCHESS. Who else will be there, officially?

PETER. The Prime Minister, I believe.

GRAND DUCHESS (*moving above the table* C *to* L *of it*) Oh, and that dear, witty Mrs Asquith. How delightful! (*She moves to the double doors, turns and looks at Mary*) Yes. I do think just a little more variety in your costume, dear. Nothing *outrée*, of course. Simply from time to time, an ordinary little day dress. Such fun it has been. Good-bye.

MARY (*with a curtsy*) Good-bye, ma'am.

(*The* GRAND DUCHESS *smiles graciously, gives the royal gesture of farewell, and exits by the double doors. The* COUNTESS *and the* BARONESS *follow her off. The doors are left open. There is a pause*)

PETER (*moving up* LC; *with a smirk*) As I am plainly *de trop*, I shall await Your Royal Highness in the hall.

(*The* REGENT *nods*)

(*To Mary*) I won't say good-bye, Miss Dagenham, as I understand I shall be seeing a lot of you in the next few days, what with special passports and other things.

MARY (*surprised*) Special passports?

REGENT (*crossing below the sofa to* C; *angrily*) Herr Gott! Northbrook. That was intended to be a surprise, and now you have utterly ruined it.

PETER. Oh. I'm so sorry, sir, but how was I to know that last night you didn't...

REGENT (*thundering*) Go, before you make things worse.

PETER. Your Royal Highness.

(PETER *backs hastily out by the double doors. The* REGENT *turns to* MARY, *who moves slowly to* R *of him*)

MARY. Good morning.

REGENT. Good morning.

(*They embrace fervently*)

My dear, I have been making such a spectacle of myself today. Behaving like a schoolboy and—this is so surprising—loving it. I see now suddenly the truth of all that you have been saying to me about the joys of childishness. It is exhilarating.

MARY (*a little sadly*) Yes, it is, isn't it? Oh dear! So this morning it's for me to be the grown-up one, is it?

REGENT. How? Grown up?

MARY. Darling—listen—you don't need to send Peter Northbrook out for a special passport. My own is quite good enough to take me to Carpathia when I come there. And what's more, my darling, I've found out the name of a good cheap pension to stay at—the *Villa Malmaison*—only just outside the city.

REGENT. But what nonsense is this? Pension? Do you not realize what I am preparing for you on your arrival?

MARY (*sadly*) No. Tell me, please. I'd love to hear.

REGENT. The Sonia Residenz, an enchanting house in the late Renaissance style—quite little—you will only need ten or fifteen servants—with a few hundred acres of park and a most beautiful garden, on a lake, with the mountains close by. It was built by a sixteenth-century ancestor of mine—for his favourite mistress...

MARY. And has been used by his twentieth-century descendant before now, huh?

REGENT. Well—(*he makes a gesture*) but never for long.

MARY. I know, my darling. (*She kisses him on the cheek*) That's just what I mean.

REGENT (*pulling her round to face him; explosively*) But Herr Gott noch mal! For not one of the others have I felt any small part of what I now feel for you.

MARY (*gently*) Yes. And for how long will you feel it, darling?
REGENT. For life.
MARY (*briskly*) Good. And so will I. You can be quite, quite sure of that. So that when my show comes off and I come out to your country and take a room at the *Villa Malmaison* and drop you a line to say that I'm there—we can go over together to the Sonia Residenz, and I can tell you what I want done to it—because if I'm going to stay in it for the rest of my time on earth, I'll need quite a lot done, won't I?

(*There is a pause. The* REGENT, *looking angry and perplexed, crosses below the chair* LC *to* L *of it*)

REGENT. When will this show of yours come off?
MARY. Oh, I'd give it another six months.
REGENT. Six months! Donner wetter, girl! Do you not realize what can happen in the world in the course of six months?
MARY (*with resigned acceptance of the facts*) Yes, darling, only too well. (*She crosses to* R *of him*) Go on, now, or you'll miss your train.
REGENT. You cannot possibly come before?
MARY. No. But thank you, my darling, so much—so very, very much, for asking me.
REGENT (*after a pause*) This is good-bye, then.
MARY. Au revoir.
REGENT. Au revoir, of course.
MARY. Of course.

(*There is a pause. A violin can be heard playing off*)

REGENT. That verdammte music. Did you order it?
MARY. No.
REGENT (*stepping away a little; savagely*) Northbrook.
MARY. Maybe.

(*They stand looking at each other for a moment*)

May I have my parting present, now, please?

(*The* REGENT *crosses to the desk, takes the brooch in its case from the drawer, returns below the sofa to* R *of Mary, and hands the case to her in silence.* MARY *takes the brooch out of its case and makes a slight scratch on it with her nail*)

REGENT. What are you doing?
MARY. Just so I'll know which one it is. (*She moves close to him*) Pin it on, please.

(*The* REGENT *pins the brooch on*)

(*She looks sadly at the top of his head*) Poor darling! Do you feel terribly disconcerted?
REGENT. Yes, I do.

(MARY *kisses him*)

MARY. Now go quickly, or I'll cry and that wouldn't be right. (*She moves to* L *of the sofa*)

(*The* REGENT *crosses to the double doors, turns, looks at her for a long time, then moves very slowly above the chair* LC. *The violin music becomes very soft*)

REGENT. Um Gottes willen! I am nearly crying myself, and that is something I have not done since I was a child.

MARY. Childishness isn't all fun, is it?

REGENT. No. (*He stares at her*)

MARY (*with a step towards him*) Anyway, my darling, whatever happens always remember this. Coming out of a heavenly dream can be a little sad, I grant, but that doesn't make the dream any the less heavenly, does it? Which is another way of saying, thank you, Your Royal Highness, from my heart. (*She curtsies*)

REGENT (*after a pause*) From my heart, too, Miss Dagenham. I believe I have as much right to that word as yourself. Perhaps more. Who knows?

(*The* REGENT *turns and exits quickly by the double doors.* MARY, *as if having forgotten something, goes to the double doors*)

MARY (*calling*) Oh, darling, I forgot to ask. Send me a photograph, please.

(*The violin music increases in volume*)

REGENT (*off; calling*) Mein Gott! What a thing to ask.

MARY (*calling*) Address it to the theatre. (*She turns away, when another thought strikes her. She calls*) And sign it.

REGENT (*off; his voice coming now very faintly*) Himmel heilige bimbaum!

(MARY *waits at the door a moment then comes back into the room and wanders over to a corner where she finds her raincoat. She puts it on. Sadly she goes to the desk where she gathers up the three identical brooch cases, and places them, one by one, in her handbag. Her two Orders of Perseverance, first and second class, follow the brooches in and the handbag is closed. Then she gathers up the two photographs and walks towards the door. Half-way there she stops, turns and looks round the room with a slight smile. Then she firmly pulls up the collar of her raincoat and walks out*)

CURTAIN

FURNITURE AND PROPERTY PLOT

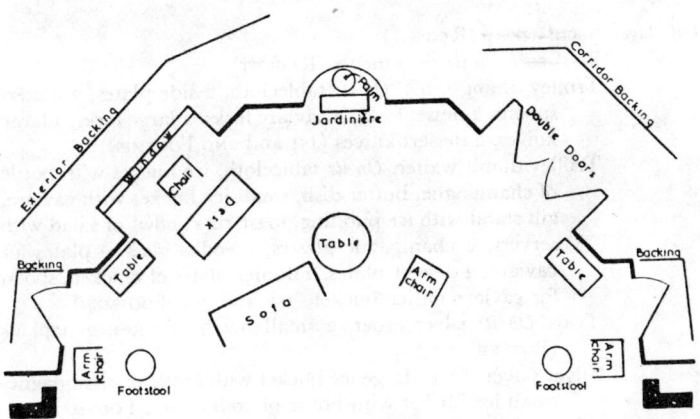

ACT I

Scene 1

On stage: Armchair (down R) *On it:* yellow cushion
~~Footstool~~
Circular table (R) *On it:* ~~table-lamp,~~ ~~clock,~~ ~~vase of flowers~~
Large desk with drawers on "on stage" side. *On it:* table-lamp, inkwell, red leather blotter, red leather notepad, pen-tray, silver rocker blotter, old-fashioned telephone, vase of flowers, ~~spectacles in case~~
In desk drawer: brooch in case, order in case
Desk chair
~~Gilt jardinière (in alcove) In it: mixed hydrangeas~~
Small circular table (in alcove) *On it:* potted palm
Sofa (RC) *On it:* 2 blue cushions, yellow cushion
Circular marble-topped table (C) *On it:* table-lamp, bell-push, ~~box with cigarettes, ashtray, matches, small silver bowl~~
~~Armchair~~ (LC)
Circular table (L) *On it:* table-lamp, magazines, vase of flowers
~~Armchair~~ (down L) ~~*On it:* yellow cushion~~
~~Footstool~~

THE SLEEPING PRINCE

Half-circular carpet on floor
~~Window curtains and pelmet~~
~~4 set triple electric candle wall-brackets~~
~~Chandelier~~
~~Doors closed~~
~~Window curtains closed~~
~~Electric fitting lit~~

Off stage: ~~Scent-spray~~ (REGENT)
~~Brief-case.~~ *In it:* documents (REGENT)
Trolley dining-table. *On it:* tablecloth, 2 side plates, 2 dessert spoons, 2 desset forks, 2 caviare forks, 2 large forks, 2 large knives, 2 dessert knives (1ST and 2ND FOOTMEN)
Trolley dumb waiter. *On it:* tablecloth, ice bucket with bottle of champagne, butter dish, small ice bucket with caviare, gilt stand with ice pudding, toast rack, bowl of salad with servers, 2 champagne glasses, 1 vodka glass, 2 plates for caviare, 2 dessert plates, 2 dinner plates of chicken, spoon for caviare on ice bucket (1ST and 2ND FOOTMEN)
Tray. *On it:* silver cruet, 2 small bowls of roses, 2 napkins (BUTLER)
Silver salver. *On it:* large ice bucket with bottle of champagne, small ice bucket with bottle of vodka (2ND FOOTMAN)
Silver salver. *On it:* 2 champagne glasses, 2 vodka glasses (1ST FOOTMAN)

Personal: REGENT: watch
MARY: handbag, gloves

SCENE 2

Strike: Mary's gloves and handbag, brief-case, documents, champagne glass from desk, dumb waiter and everything on it, salver, ice buckets, glasses and silver bowl from table C

Set: On table C: tablecloth, clean silver ash bowl, carafe of water, glass
On left arm of sofa: newspapers

Re-set: ~~Footstools in front of chair down L~~
Tidy desk
~~Double doors open~~
~~Doors down R and L closed~~
~~Window curtains open~~
~~Electric fittings out~~

Off stage: List of names (REGENT)
~~Bedspread~~ (~~MARY~~)

THE S~~

   Tray. *On it:* 2 breakfast cup~~
       jug of hot milk, sugar bas~~
   Raincoat to fit Mary (PETER)
   Jewel chest. *In it:* pearl choker, diam~~
   Paper with telephone number (NICOLAS)

Personal: MARY: handbag

ACT II

SCENE 1

Strike: Tablecloth, coffee set and cup, silver ash bowl from table C, newspapers from sofa, jewel chest from chair behind desk

Set: ~~Footstool from down R to below right end of sofa~~
   Book ~~on footstool~~
   Box of chocolates on floor below left end of sofa
   Mary's handbag on table C
   ~~Silver ash bowl on table C~~

Re-set: Brooch and case in ~~desk drawer~~ BUREAU
   Put desk chair under desk
~~Doors closed~~
~~Window curtains open~~
~~Electric fittings out~~

Off stage: Pack of cards (LOUISA)

SCENE 2

Strike: Book and playing cards from desk
   Chocolates from table C

Set: Dumb waiter (up C) *On it:* tablecloth, ice bucket with bottle of champagne, butter dish, small ice bucket with caviare, gilt stand with ice pudding, toast rack, bowl of salad with servers, 2 champagne glasses, 1 vodka glass, 2 plates for caviare, 2 dessert plates, 2 dinner plates of chicken, spoon for caviare on ice bucket
   On table C: salver with large ice bucket and bottle of champagne, small ice bucket and bottle of vodka, 2 vodka glasses

Re-set: Brooch and case in ~~desk drawer~~ BUREAU
   ~~Footstool in front of chair down R~~

THE SLEEPING PRINCE

~~Doors closed~~
~~Window curtains closed~~
~~Electric fittings lit~~

Personal: MARY: handbag. *In it:* manifesto, piece of crumpled paper

SCENE 3

Strike: Dumb waiter and everything on it
Salver, ice buckets, glasses, ~~silver ash bowl~~ from table C
Document from desk

Set: On *table* C: tablecloth, pot of coffee, jug of hot milk, sugar basin with tongs, 2 breakfast cups and saucers, 2 spoons, silver ash bowl with water (for putting out letter)

Re-set: ~~Footstool in front of chair down L~~
~~Double doors open~~
~~Doors down R and L closed~~
~~Window curtains open~~
~~Electric fittings out~~

Off stage: Letter (PETER)
Brooch in case (NICOLAS)
Photograph (NICOLAS)
Photograph (BARONESS)

Personal: COUNTESS: handbag. *In it:* brooch in case, handkerchief

LIGHTING PLOT

Property fittings required: ~~chandelier, 4 table-lamps, 4 sets triple electric candle wall-brackets~~

Interior. A reception room. The same scene throughout

The MAIN ACTING AREAS are at a chair (LC), a sofa (RC) and a desk (R)

ACT I, SCENE 1. Evening

The APPARENT SOURCES OF LIGHT are a ~~chandelier C; wall-brackets R, up RC, up LC and L;~~ ~~table-lamps~~ R, up R, C and L

To open: Effect of bright electric lighting
Fittings on
Flood outside double doors, on
Strips outside doors R and L, on

Cue 1   ~~The REGENT switches off the wall-brackets~~   (Page 24)
       ~~Snap out wall-brackets~~
       ~~Reduce general lighting~~

Cue 2   ~~The REGENT switches off the chandelier~~   (Page 24)
       ~~Snap out chandelier~~
       ~~Reduce general lighting~~

Cue 3   ~~The REGENT switches off the table-lamp L~~   (Page 24)
       ~~Snap out table-lamp~~ L
       ~~Reduce lighting~~ L

Cue 4   ~~The REGENT switches off the table-lamp R~~   (Page 25)
       ~~Snap out table-lamp~~ R
       ~~Reduce lighting~~ R

ACT I, SCENE 2. Morning

~~The APPARENT SOURCE OF LIGHT is a large window~~ R

To open: Effect of summer sunshine
Fittings off
Flood outside double doors, on
Strips outside doors R and L, on

No cues

ACT II, SCENE 1. Early evening

To open: Effect of evening sunshine
Fittings off
Flood outside double doors, on
Strips outside doors R and L, on

No cues

ACT II, SCENE 2. Night

To open: Effect of bright electric lighting
Fittings on
Flood outside double doors, on
Strips outside doors R and L, on

Cue 5   MARY switches out the table-lamp L   (Page 70)
Snap out table-lamp L
Reduce lighting L

ACT II, SCENE 3. Morning

To open: Effect of summer sunshine
Fittings off
Flood outside double doors, on
Strips outside doors R and L, on

Cue 6   PETER: Your Royal Highness   (Page 80)
Reduce on-stage lighting a little on a two-minute check